Longing for Heaven

*A Devotional Look
at the Life After Death*

Peter Toon

Macmillan Publishing Company
New York

Macmillan Publishing Company
866 Third Avenue, New York, NY 10022

Library of Congress Cataloging-in-Publication Data
Toon, Peter, 1939–
    Longing for heaven: a devotional look at the life after death/
Peter Toon.
        p.   cm.
    Bibliography: p.
    ISBN 0-02-619541-0
    1. Heaven—Christianity.   2. Spiritual life—Anglican authors.
I. Title.
BT846.2.T66   1989
236′.24—dc19   88-31167
                        CIP

Macmillan books are available at special discounts for bulk purchases for sales promotions, premiums, fund-raising, or educational use. For details, contact:

Special Sales Director
Macmillan Publishing Company
866 Third Avenue
New York, NY 10022

10 9 8 7 6 5 4 3 2 1

Printed in the United States of America

For
Thomas Arthur and Doris Toon
(in England)
and
Don and Dottie Reiner
(in America)

Contents

Foreword * ix
Preface * xi

Introduction * 1

PART I

1. My Father, Your Father * 13
2. Heaven: Past, Present, Future * 25
3. Treasure in Heaven * 37
4. Patient Hope * 53
5. A Better Country * 73
6. A Living and Purifying Hope * 86

PART II

7. Obstacles and Hindrances * 97
8. Meditation: What Is It? * 107

Contents * viii

9. Practical Benefits * 127

Epilogue * 135

Notes * 143

Foreword

Those who try to communicate the Christian faith in our secular age face a difficulty which, though present in some degree through the history of the Church, is particularly acute today. On the one hand, we have to resist the temptation to restrict the Gospel to the spiritual realm and deny its application for the whole of life, including that of society. On the other hand, if we are to be faithful to the teaching of the New Testament, we must also insist that man is created not merely for life in this world in our space and time, but for eternal fellowship with the living God.

If we emphasize the former point, we may well be accused of ignoring the eternal destiny of man and of implying that the real purpose of the Gospel is to enable us to be happier simply in terms of a life from birth to death. If we emphasize the latter point, we shall probably be accused of being escapist and of evading the "real" problems of life which people face day by day and which we meet in society. The pressure upon us to think primarily in terms of this world alone is evident in the fact that when the eternal dimension is given place, it is often justified on the grounds of its usefulness in facing our earthly problems.

Dr. Toon faces this situation in a positive and constructive way. He does not simply affirm the eternal destiny of man, though he does point out that "the more intensely the hope of being with Christ in heaven burns in our hearts, the more vigorously do we love our neighbor and experience the foretaste of heaven in celebratory worship." He recognizes that much of our trouble springs from our vague and unsatisfying vision of heaven. He is, therefore, concerned to give it content, and this he does in a deeply Scriptural and refreshing way. His approach is in no way escapist, though he points out that heavenly-mindedness, which is "a necessary part of the Christian outlook and approach to life and death," does enable us, by setting this world and things in it against the heavenly world where Christ is enthroned, to come to a "proper evaluation of the things of this world."

Dr. Toon points out that, notwithstanding the theological bias of our time to a this-worldly Gospel, the number appears to be growing of those who "want to believe in heaven as that holy Reality above and beyond all that is and upon which our universe is dependent." I believe he is right and his book will do much to enable that desire to be fulfilled, not least because in Part II he gives some very practical advice as to how our vision of heaven, soundly rooted in Scripture, can be achieved.

Graham Leonard
The Bishop of London

Preface

You may like to know why I wrote this book, which is a new departure for me in that most of my previous books have been of the nature of historical or theological studies. I would want to classify this under the general heading of Christian Spirituality. So it is addressed not merely to the intelligence but via the mind to the heart and will. This explains why I have few footnotes. I do not want my readers to be diverted into interesting issues and scholarly contributions to them; rather, I want them to be ready to receive what I have to say—if they judge it to be true—with their whole souls in order to be faithful to the Lord.

Having written two textbooks for American seminary students on heaven (*The Ascension of Our Lord*, 1984, and *Heaven and Hell*, 1986, both released by Thomas Nelson Publishers), I came to realize that a missing element in much contemporary piety and spirituality is the *longing* to be with Christ in the heavenly realm and to participate in his glory. Much of what I want to say about this theme has been said before. It has been well said by Richard Baxter (1615–1691) in his eminently readable *The Saints' Everlasting Rest*; by John Owen (1616–1683) in *The Grace and Duty of Being Spiritually-Minded*; and by Bishop Joseph Hall (1574–1656) in his *The Art of Divine Meditation*, itself inspired by various medieval books on spirituality. And long before any of these writers, it had been said by the great Augustine of Hippo (354–430) in his *City of God*. So I am not saying anything new. I am trying to present what has always been regarded over the long centuries as a necessary aspect of Christian faith and practice.

I am grateful to David Wavre and Carolyn Armitage of Hodders for their help and advice, and I am grateful to my former teacher, Dr. Eric Mascall, for introducing me to the profound thoughts of St. Augustine on heaven.

The Bishop of London, well known both for his orthodoxy and kindness, kindly agreed to write a Foreword. I thank him for identifying with me in the call for heavenly-mindedness in the Church.

Peter Toon
Advent Sunday, 1985

Introduction

This book is for those who, recognizing that heaven exists, do not, or cannot as yet, take this belief seriously.

Certainly, all Christians profess to believe in heaven, for it is part of the general content of belief recited in the Apostles' and Nicene Creeds; but not all apparently feel that they ought to believe in God's heaven with any obvious intensity or personal commitment. However, the number appears to be growing of those who really and truly want to believe in heaven as that holy Reality 'above and beyond all that is and upon which our universe is dependent. It is for that number that this book is written. I am inviting people to come on a journey with me to explore what we mean by heaven and to ascertain what we ought to be doing about its existence.

Not a Geographical Task

Heaven cannot be described as if it were like a delightful foreign country encouraging tourists and emigrants to go there. Not only do we not have any videos, photographs or media reports of it, but also we have no travel directions on how to get there. Though heaven may certainly be "glimpsed," partially known, experienced and longed for by spiritually minded people on this earth, it may not be reached by any of our senses. The route is spiritual, since heaven is not part of our space and time. Going there is not like going from America to China or from California to the moon.

The incarnation of the Son of God was not a journey from outer space to our earth to become Jesus of Nazareth, and the Ascension of Jesus was not a journey from our earth into outer space to sit upon a throne in a distant planet. The Incarnation was a movement or transfer from an invisible world with its own space and time into our visible universe, and the Ascension was a movement or transfer from our space and time into an invisible world with a different space and time. Therefore, heaven is near, but the nearness cannot be measured in miles or kilometers. It is inaccessible to us via our present physical bodies with their sinful natures. This means that all our descriptions of the invisible world have to be via images, symbols and metaphors. Using such language, we talk of heaven as being "up there" and "above the skies": we probably mean that heaven is beyond our reach and that this world is dependent upon that world. Since heaven is not part of our universe, we cannot get help from cosmology to find it: access to heaven now must be via the Holy

Spirit, who belongs to the invisible realm and who comes from there to here in order to dwell within faithful believers. The Holy Spirit brings heaven and Christ to us, and through his ministry we alone experience heaven. However, after death—and certainly after the general resurrection of the dead at Christ's second coming—we shall be in heaven to see, know and enjoy God forever.

Not an Easy Task

To believe in, and to long for, heaven are particularly difficult spiritual and moral exercises in our Western world. This is because we find it difficult to shake our human spirits free from the view that this material world (which modern science and technology are slowly mastering) is effectively the only real and true world, and thus from the further suspicion that heaven is, at best, secondary and, at worst, nonexistent or superfluous! To make matters worse, our normal way of viewing this world is dominated by scientific knowledge, and thus we have lost the art of seeing God revealed in and through his creation.

For people two centuries ago, the vision of God available within the natural order seems to have been the normal way to see the world, but, for us, that way is now apparently unnatural and odd. Thus we have a double problem—we hardly see God revealed in his universe and we, therefore, do not easily think of this world as itself dependent upon that other world of heaven, where God uniquely dwells and is wholly known and experienced by his creatures.

All this has its effects upon the way in which God is known, worshipped and experienced by many Christians today. Because our apprehension of the vision of God in nature is poor and dim, and because the longing to be in heaven with Jesus is weak and unstable (except perhaps among the believing elderly who wish to die), there is a tendency to confuse the longing of the heart for heaven with that foretaste of heaven which is genuinely experienced within dynamic Christian fellowship, worship, prayer and service here and now. This tendency to equate the taste of the Reality with the Reality itself appears to be common within house-churches and charismatically renewed groups where there is genuine experience of God in and through the ministry of the Spirit. This experience ought to create a longing for the wholeness of knowing, seeing and experiencing God in the face of Jesus Christ; but because of the pressure of our day, it can become an end in itself (especially when tied to affluent, middle-class life-styles). And as such it is dangerous.

Perhaps an illustration will help clarify this point. Take, for example, the British Embassy Cultural Centre and Anglican Cathedral in the city of Seoul, South Korea. To live, work and worship in that context may be interpreted as enjoying a taste of the much larger experience of living, working and worshipping in Britain. The British ethos is there in Seoul but is trapped within a Korean context; for only in Britain is the British ethos truly and wholly known. Thus the British family in Seoul longs for home and family while also enjoying life in Seoul. And, in the same way the Bible teaches us in Colossians 3:1–3, and Hebrews 3:1, that the disciples of Jesus Christ are to long for the heavenly realm where Christ is while enjoying the presence of God within the created order, within the community of disciples and within the individual heart. Of course, this is easily said but is achieved only with difficulty.

The people in the Embassy in Seoul have memories of Britain, and these are strengthened as they receive information and get news from visitors from the homeland; but the people of God on earth have no memories of heaven and welcome no guests from there. They do, however, have the presence of the indwelling Spirit who comes in the name of, and from, the exalted Lord Jesus, and they do possess the promises of God recorded in the sacred Scriptures. This means that their lives ought to be characterized by faith and hope—virtues which can be diluted or polluted by the highly secularist society in which we live.

The problem of a weak longing for, and minimal interest in, heaven will not be—indeed cannot be—solved by activism, dashing here and there in the name of the Lord. For unless the Christian's gaze and orientation are heavenward, activity is so much like running round in circles and getting only to places in the circle. Thus the problem needs to be faced before activity is actually begun, in order that activity be rightly motivated and directed. While we must recognize that no single method or way will wholly restore or create the genuine longing for the heavenly realm where Christ is, the conviction will be expressed in this book that meditation upon, and contemplation of, heaven ought to be encouraged and practiced within the Christian community as a well-tried and successful way of moving in the right direction.

Obviously, we cannot meditate on heaven until we

have some information from which to begin and we cannot contemplate heaven until we have some thoughts to develop. Thus the first and major part of this book will be a series of studies of the place of heaven in the teaching and experience of Jesus and of his apostles; it will be emphasized that heaven is both "above" and "to come," and in each case heaven is what it is for us because of Jesus. And the second and shorter part will offer encouragement to meditation and contemplation on God's heaven.

Before these tasks are begun, it is necessary that we be aware of the right method to adopt in our work of study and reflection. We shall contrast two approaches in order to accept one and reject the other. These may be represented as (a) that of the spectator who looks on from the outside with genuine interest, and (b) that of the player who is fully involved in the game.

Not a Spectator

Temptations come to us in every area of life. We cannot escape them. One temptation facing those who would seek to know about God and his heaven is merely to become a student of eschatology (*eschatos* = end; *logos* = study). There are many books on theology which include a chapter on what is expected at the end of the age—the second coming of Christ, the resurrection of the dead, and the final judgment—and what will follow—the kingdom of God in a new order of creation, focused on, and determined by, heaven.[1] There are other books which trace the development of the doctrine of immortality and bodily resurrection from the

Old Testament via the intertestamental literature of Judaism into the New Testament.[2] And, of course, there is a host of controversial material on whether or not there will be a millennial reign of Christ and his saints on earth before the end of this age.[3]

Another temptation is to get too deeply involved in the perennial debates concerning whether or not the human being survives death as a disembodied self or whether or not human beings possess immortal souls, or how the relation of time to eternity is to be expressed.[4]

Let us be clear. The temptation is on the one hand merely to become a student of eschatology or on the other hand to be too deeply involved in intellectual questioning. It is certainly good to be a student of eschatology and to face serious intellectual questions; however, from a Christian perspective, these must surely contribute to a longing to be with Christ in heaven and to do his will here on earth. If they are an end in themselves, they may be interesting or fascinating, depressive or stimulating, but they are not genuinely Christian pursuits. The intellect, heart and will must function together for the glory of God. Discussing, debating and studying theological topics, if divorced from the life of prayer and worship and not a part of the Christian pilgrimage, can actually be the means of a drawing away from communion with God.

Therefore, our attitude must not only be "I believe in order to understand," but also, "I believe, trust and obey in order to understand." Or to put it another way, I cannot merely say, "I think, therefore I am," but rather, as a pilgrim, I need to say, "I struggle, therefore I am." Thus the attitude we ought to have is not that of the spectator who merely looks on with interest; rather, it is that of the player who is wholly involved in the game. Perhaps a brief personal testimony will not be out of place.

Some people have flashes of insight and then are convinced of the truth of what they have seen, other people come to a conclusion slowly through a complex route of experience and reflection. I came to the conclusion that much contemporary Christian spirituality lacked a longing for the heavenly realm, where Christ is, over a period of time. The last part of that route may be dated to 1983, when I gave the W. H. Griffith Thomas Lectures in Dallas, Texas, on "The Ascension of Jesus, the Christ." Preparation of these caused me to realize not only that there had been little written on the Ascension of our Lord in modern times, but that many Christians did not appear to be conscious that they were to set their minds and hearts on Christ, who is above at the right hand of the Father. The publisher of my work on the Ascension then invited me to write on "Heaven and Hell," for, here again, very little had been published in modern times. The fact that so little had been published on heaven at either the popular or serious level during the last fifty years naturally caused me to think that preaching on heaven and longing for heaven were not as common as they ought to be within Western Christendom. Then I recalled my earlier historical studies in the seventeenth century and my reading of the writings of the great English Anglican, Puritan and Nonconformist divines. In their books the fact of heaven, and the longing to be there with Jesus, were powerfully expressed. Further, I rediscovered just how important for them was the practice of meditation (including meditation upon the exalted Jesus and heaven) in their spirituality and piety. All this occurred as I completed my book *Heaven and Hell* for Thomas Nelson Publishers of America.

As I researched and reflected, I also was involved as a minister in preaching and teaching. I taught a course in 1985 in the Reformed Theological Seminary, Jackson, Mississippi, on "Heaven and Spirituality" which was a historical overview; further, I preached in various churches and colleges in both the U.S.A. and Britain on the topic of heaven and our duty to set our minds on Christ who is above. Naturally, I talked to people and made observations, and as I did this, I came to the painful conclusion that longing for the heavenly realm appeared to play little direct part in modern spirituality, be it of the charismatic, the evangelical or the traditional kind. Where I observed enthusiasm and commitment, I also observed that, while enjoying the presence of the gifts and graces of the Holy Spirit (who came to them from the exalted Lord Jesus), those involved appeared to be satisfied with the combination of their affluent life-style and their "taste" of heaven. Seemingly, the taste of heaven was so good—within the context of the benefits of Western civilization—that to have the real thing in its wholeness was not felt necessary. Further, there was little or no direct preaching on heaven and the exalted Jesus to encourage any longing to be with Christ in his glory.

To be personal, I found that while I was conscious of the powerful theme within the New Testament for developing heavenly-mindedness and while I had studied what the saints of the past had written on longing for heaven, I, too, had only a minimal longing for heaven in order to commune with, and to be with, the

Lord Jesus. It became clear to me that I ought to become less earthly minded and more heavenly minded, not to become less useful on earth but to become more useful for the kingdom of God! Further, I came to recognize that to study what the Scriptures say about heaven (which is extremely important), to be diligent and sincere in prayer to God who is in heaven (which is extremely important) and to be faithful in attendance at divine worship and in the receiving of the sacramental body and blood of Christ in Holy Communion (which is extremely important) are not enough of themselves to cultivate that heavenly-mindedness which is pleasing to our Lord. This is because God has appointed a further way, a way that is much neglected these days, and that is the way of meditation or contemplation. I am using these two words as synonyms in this book, although I recognize that they can be used of different forms of the one exercise.

If by study we seek to learn the truth, and if by prayer we seek to have communion with God, then by meditation or contemplation we seek to order our thoughts in such a way that they affect our hearts and wills to desire and to go after that which we judge to be desirable. Meditation should cause us to love and delight in that which we consider to be the way of the Lord. The discipline of meditation has never been easy and it gets less easy in our busy world. But I know of no other way to develop our spirituality in the direction commanded by our Lord. Therefore, we ought to attempt it and to do so regularly.

PART I

1. My Father, Your Father

"Blessed are the pure in heart for they will see God"—who eternally exists as Father, Son and Holy Spirit. The pure in heart enjoy full communion and loving fellowship with God, whom they see and know in, through and with the Lord Jesus, who is the Son Incarnate.

God is One—there is one Godhead—deity—and yet God is also a Trinity of Persons. Within the One Being of God there is plurality; within the Godhead there is a fellowship and a communion of Persons. God is holy love, and as a Trinity of Persons, the Father loves the Son and the Son loves the Father within the bond of union who is the Holy Spirit. The pure in heart participate in this holy love because their Savior and Lord, in and by whom they come to God, is himself a Participant. Our calling as disciples is to be drawn by the Lord

Jesus in the power of the Holy Spirit into the eternal, holy love of God himself.

Faithful believers of the old covenant recognized that their true purpose was to do the will of the Lord and enter into his presence to glorify his name and receive his blessing. Here is how one psalmist addressed God: "Yet I am always with you; you hold me by my right hand. You guide me with your counsel, and afterwards you will take me into glory. Whom have I in heaven but you? And being with you I desire nothing on earth. My flesh and my heart may fail, but God is the strength of my heart and my portion for ever" (Ps. 73:23–26).

Faithful believers of the new covenant have the same purpose but are privileged to have a clearer knowledge of what this entails and how it is gained. Believers of the old covenant looked forward in hope for the arrival of the Messiah: we look up in faith to the Messiah in heaven and we look back via the Gospels to receive his word. We believe that he is the same yesterday, today and forever because not only is he God's Messiah or Christ, but he is also the eternal Son who took to himself our flesh and nature so that, without ceasing to be God, he also became one of us. Thus he is the Incarnate Son.

Incarnate Son

Jesus began his ministry as Messiah after John the Baptist had prepared the way. In fact, Jesus received Baptism at the hands of John as he committed himself to the cause of God's righteousness. According to Mark's account of the Baptism, Jesus had a vision as he came up out of the water. "He saw heaven being torn open and the Spirit descending on him like a dove. And a voice came from heaven: 'You are my Son, whom I love; with you I am well pleased' '' (Mk. 1:10–11). Mark makes it clear that only Jesus saw this vision and heard the voice of God.[1] It is instructive to compare this experience of Jesus, which became the moment for the inauguration of his public ministry, with the way in which the prophets of the old covenant received their call. They received a message and a mission, a word and a task. What Jesus experienced and received was not in the first place a message and a mission but a sense of status with, and relation to, the LORD. With Jesus, who and what he is precede what he does and what he says. His word and works are important, but they flow from his identity and, particularly, his relation to the LORD.

Thus Jesus was a prophet but more than a prophet, and on several occasions in the Gospels there are indications that he was fully conscious of the way in which he differed from the great prophets. His remarks about John the Baptist (Mt. 11:11–13; Lk. 7:28; 16:16) point in this direction, he also does the parable of the tenants of the vineyard, who killed the messengers (prophets) and then proceeded to treat the Son in the same way (Mk. 12:1–12). Jesus knew that he stood in a special, indeed a unique, relation to the LORD. We believe that he was, and remains, the Incarnate Son.

Perhaps our understanding of Jesus as Incarnate Son will be helped by reading carefully the great theological definition of his Person produced by the Council of Chalcedon in 451. Here it is in a modern paraphrase:

However you choose to express, in expounding the Christian faith in Christ, your interpretation of Jesus, say nothing of him that indicates or implies that he is any less God than the Father is God: and say nothing of him that indicates or implies that he is any less human than we ourselves are— except that he is not a sinner, as we are. But remember above all that it is in Jesus that we believe God to be revealed—not as if Jesus merely mediates a revelation of God, but because he himself reveals God by being who he is, in his very personhood. So you must say nothing of him that indicates or implies that he is other than God in person or that he has some kind of dual personality.[2]

We speak of Jesus, Incarnate Son, as one Person, with two natures (one human, one divine), and we confess that how he is so is a mystery—a truth we can never wholly fathom.

Because Jesus is who he is, we look to him as our representative, living, dying and rising for us, and our substitute, doing for us what we cannot do for ourselves. Further, because he is truly Man we look to him as our example, showing us how human life is to be lived. Not only is he the one who reveals God to us and saves us, he is also the one who tells us to follow him and do as he does. Certainly, we cannot imitate his work as Messiah and Redeemer, but we can imitate his single-minded devotion to the LORD and his intimate fellowship with heaven.

We believe that he passed through all the stages of growth from infancy through boyhood to manhood and faced all the common temptations that we face. We believe that he had to exercise personal discipline and to train his will to accord with the will of God. As a boy of twelve he was precocious and seemed to have a special sense of communion with the Lord (Lk. 2:49), but this did not lessen his need as Man to develop his relationship with heaven. Thus it is Jesus in his real manhood who provides for us the example of longing for the heavenly realm.

God, the Father

In this chapter we shall observe how, as Man, the Incarnate Son enjoyed intimate communion with God and longed for the time when that communion would not be restricted by finite and temporal existence but would be expressed in the freedom and magnitude of heaven. This is intimately bound up in the relationship between Jesus and the LORD which is characterized by the use of the name "Father." In Christian worship and discourse we have become so used to calling God "Father" that it is easy to forget or ignore the fact that for Jesus and the first Christians to call God "Father" was the heart of their communion with, and service of, God. Thus we must look at the way Jesus used the name "Father," but before doing this, and to set it in context, we need to look briefly into the Old Testament and Jewish tradition to see how the name was used there.

One thing must be made clear. When using the word "Father," the Jewish writers did not intend to suggest that the biological aspect of fatherhood was being indicated. Their emphasis was on the other aspect of fatherhood, that of being responsible for the welfare of the children and the family. Therefore, God is presented as the Father of the people Israel because, first of all, he adopted them as his special people (Dt. 32:6; Is. 63:16; Mal. 2:10) and, secondly, because he has constant care for them (Dt. 1:31; 8:5; Is. 1:2). In turn, they are expected to behave as trusting and obedient children

(Dt. 14:1; Je. 3:19; Mal. 1:6). So, those Israelites who do seek to be faithful to their covenant LORD truly know God as their Father (Ps. 103:13; Mal. 3:17). This usage is also expressed in the Jewish literature produced in the century before Jesus was born and the one in which he lived. But did individual Jews in private prayer actually address God as Father? If any Jew did this, then he was stepping outside the tradition which normally only allowed God to be addressed as "Father" in collective prayers (see, e.g., Jer. 3:4, 19; Is. 63:16; 64:8).

When we turn to the four Gospels, we find that Jesus is presented as addressing God as "my Father," and as doing so when praying.[3] This remarkable unanimity gives us confidence to follow Jeremias and claim that Jesus addressed God in the Aramaic, " 'Abbā."[4] This word, used by both younger and older children of their father in the Jewish homes of Palestine, was an intimate term and, as far as we know, was not used at all in the prayers in the synagogue or temple. Though the New Testament is written in Greek, it is remarkable that 'Abbā has been retained in three places (Mk. 14:36 [" 'Abbā, Father"]; Rom. 8:15; Gal. 4:6), thereby pointing to the importance of this word in the oral tradition concerning Jesus and in the experience of the first converts in the Gentile world.

"The complete novelty and uniqueness of 'Abbā as an address to God in the prayers of Jesus shows that it expresses the heart of Jesus' relation to God. He spoke to God as a child to its father: confidently and securely, and yet at the same time reverently and obediently."[5] 'Abbā was for him a sacred word and thus he taught his disciples to use it with care: "Do not call anyone on earth 'father' for you have one Father, and he is in heaven" (Mt. 23:9). Jesus was not forbidding the calling of physical fathers by the name "father." He was thinking of the custom of addressing rabbis and distinguished people as " '*Abbā*," for this was the name by which he addressed God and the name he was teaching them also to use for God—as in "Our Father . . ."

Jesus was conscious of being authorized by God to communicate his self-revelation to the Jews and the world. His filial consciousness, confirmed to him at the Baptism, was expressed in the way he addressed God as "my Father" —" '*Abbā*." This is seen in a prayer of Jesus found in Matthew 11:25–7 and Luke 10:21–2.

> I praise you, Father, Lord of heaven and earth, because you have hidden these things from the wise and learned, and revealed them to little children. Yes, Father, for this was your good pleasure.
>
> All things have been committed to me by my Father. No one knows the Son except the Father, and no one knows the Father except the Son and those to whom the Son chooses to reveal him.

The duty of a father in Judaism was to initiate his son into the words of the Torah as well as into the secrets of his craft or trade. Whatever the father knew he had a responsibility to pass on to his son and not to anyone else. In a similar manner Jesus, as Son, has received special, secret communication from his Father; thus, as a consequence, he can now reveal the Father in a way that no one else can possibly do. Further, when people become his disciples, he imparts to them this revelation and thus, in dependence upon him, they can address God as " '*Abbā*" also. However, they can never have an identical relationship with the Father as that of the Son; at all times their " '*Abbā*" is dependent upon his. Though he can, and does, join with them in the synagogue to recite the prayers—e.g., "Blessed art Thou, LORD, God of Abraham . . ."—he can never say with them "Our Father . . ." To do so would make him an adopted son rather than the only-begotten, eternal Son of the Father. His Sonship is from everlasting to everlasting and is therefore unique: neither angel nor man can possess such a filial relation.

Based on his study of the use of "Father" in the first three Gospels, T. W. Manson has written: "The Father is the supreme reality in the life of Jesus. His experience of the Father is something so profound and so moving that it will not bear to be spoken about except to those who have shown themselves to be fitted to hear. At the same time it shines through his words and deeds in such wise that those who see him see the Father. By what he is he makes the Father real to men."[6] In a later chapter we shall examine how he makes the Father real to his disciples. Here we must move into the Gospel of John, where the relationship of Jesus, as Son, is prominent.

There has been much discussion as to whether or not the words placed on the lips of Jesus by the author of John's Gospel are authentic. My own view is that this teaching is an adaptation of the informal teaching which Jesus gave to his disciples when the crowds had gone and which, in fact, made little sense to them until after the Resurrection and Ascension of Jesus and the descent of the Spirit. Thus it is teaching which will have been remembered and interpreted in the light of the Resurrection. However, this in no way affects its veracity. In fact, for our purposes, it fills out the "my Father" of Matthew, Mark and Luke.

At the end of the marvelous prologue of John's Gospel, the One who has been described as the eternal Word who became flesh is now called "the one and only Son" (Jn. 1:14). And from this point to the end of the Gospel, the relation of the Father and the Son becomes a major theme. In fact, John uses the term "Father" for God more than twice as often as the other writers of Gospels. Of the Son we learn the following.

1. *He is the unique and only Son of the Father.*   Jesus was conscious that as Son he had a preexistence before his birth of Mary: "Before Abraham was born, I am" (8:58). And John explained that in love of the world "God gave his one and only Son" (3:16). Thus Jesus as Son enjoyed a unique filial consciousness.

2. *He is united to the Father in holy love* (agapē).   "The Father loves the Son and has placed everything in his hands" (3:35). This divine love is the very love which through Jesus is directed to his disciples: "As the Father has loved me, so have I loved you. Now remain in my love" (15:9). God's love (*agapē*) is only possessed by God and is only present in human beings through the Son and by the Spirit.

3. *He is one in being or essence with the Father.*   "I and the Father are one," claimed Jesus (10:30). "One" is neuter and thus points to what they have in common, which is more than aims and objectives: it is "being." On another occasion Jesus put their unity in another way: "The Father is in me and I am in the Father" (10:38; cf. 14:10–11, 20).

4. *He has been sent from heaven to earth by the Father.* On several occasions Jesus spoke of the "Father who sent me" (5:37; 12:49) and of coming "in my Father's name" (5:43). Jesus was conscious that he had entered into our space and time from a different sphere, that of heaven.

5. As the One sent by the Father, he does the will and works of the Father and also speaks his words. "My food," said Jesus, "is to do the will of him who sent me and to finish his work" (4:34). And concerning what he taught, Jesus claimed: "My teaching is not my own. It comes from him who sent me" (7:16). Also he said: "He who sent me is reliable, and what I have heard from him I tell the world" (8:26).

6. He is inferior to the Father in the same way that a messenger is inferior to the One who sent him on his task. In his farewell discourse Jesus told the disciples: "If you loved me you would be glad that I am going to the Father, for the Father is greater than I" (14:28). This text has been used to claim that the Son is subordinate in being to the Father; however, that of which it speaks is a subordination of purpose, for at the level of activity (rather than being) he who sends is greater than he who, having been sent, is returning to the one who sent him.

7. He returns to the Father as the one and only Son and in possession of the flesh he has assumed. Before his arrest Jesus told his friends: "I came from the Father and entered the world: now I am leaving the world and going back to the Father" (16:28). In fact, after his Resurrection, as he was on his way from earth to heaven, he met Mary and told her: "I am returning to my Father and your Father, to my God and your God" (20:17). Here the Son in his resurrected and glorified body is still maintaining the distinction of relationships with the Father; his own is the primary one and that of his disciples is a dependent one.

8. He will ask the Father to send the Holy Spirit from heaven to the waiting disciples on earth. "I will ask the Father, and he will give you another counselor to be with you forever—the Spirit of truth" (14:16). Jesus himself is their first Paraclete (here translated, counselor, but also advocate, or friend who stands alongside to help), and the Holy Spirit, coming in the name of Jesus to them, will be their second, replacing the first on earth but not in heaven. This Paraclete will teach them all things and remind them of everything that Jesus has said to them (14:26).

9. *He will return to earth at the end of the age as Judge of the world.* (5:22, 26, 27)

10. *He is the One through whom the Father gives salvation and eternal life.* (3:16, 18, 36; 5:21, 24)

As you carefully reflect upon these claims concerning the relationship of the Father and the Son, as well as of the Holy Spirit to each of them, you find yourself entering the basis for the Christian doctrine of the Holy Trinity. However, you also find yourself asking questions as to the unique self-consciousness and filial consciousness of Jesus. As you ponder these matters, you will probably come to a conclusion such as the following, which has great bearing upon our belief that Jesus is our example.

As the Word made flesh and the Son incarnate, Jesus had a unique filial consciousness, which was composed of two parts. As eternal Son he always possesses a divine mode of consciousness of unity with the Father within the holy love of the Trinity; but from his incarnation he also has possessed a human mode of consciousness as Man. Thus the mysterious and complex filial consciousness of Jesus is not one that we can imitate. However, we can imitate that which he experienced in his human mode of consciousness, which was intimately related to his life of prayer and praise, trust and obedience, in the service of the Father. As Man, Jesus had an intimate communion with the Father and longed for that communion to reach its fullness in heaven. And this is what we also ought to have and long for.

In the prayer of John 17, Jesus also asked: "Father, glorify me in your presence with the glory I had with you before the world began" (v. 5). He spoke here as the Incarnate Son (one Person with two natures), and thus the glory to which he is to be reinstated is a glory that will encompass his human nature. Thus Jesus, as Man, will in his resurrection body enjoy to the fullest possible degree that communion with God of which created and perfected human nature is capable. What he enjoyed to the full in the restricting conditions of earthly space and time, he will now enjoy in a greater and richer fullness in the expansive conditions of heavenly space and time. In the next chapter, which describes heaven, the place, position and reward of Jesus as exalted Man will be discussed.

Some might think that it would be more logical (or just better) in the next chapter to look at the teaching of Jesus concerning communion with the Father, with its inbuilt longing for the heavenly realm. However, is it not the case that the Church over the centuries has accepted the teaching of Jesus as divine because it first accepted that he was raised from the dead and taken up into heaven? Therefore, after we have viewed Christ "above" and also "to come," we shall look at his teaching, in order to receive it as the word of the living, exalted Lord from heaven, communicated to us by his Spirit.

2. Heaven: Past, Present, Future

God created the heavens as part of the physical universe. He created heaven as the sphere in which created beings who possess immortality would dwell. We can see the heavens but we cannot see heaven; yet we believe that both are the direct creation of the Lord. God ordained that the visible world in which we live should be subordinate to, and dependent upon, the invisible world in which the angels live. The heavens will not last forever, for as part of the physical universe, they are scheduled in God's plan to disappear at the end of the present evil age. In contrast, heaven will last forever, since God has ordained that it will ever be the sphere where created beings with immortality enjoy his presence and blessing.

In ancient as well as in modern times, many people have believed that heaven is above or through the heavens. Yet they have held also that heaven is of a very different nature from the heavens. Today, in the light of modern physics and cosmology, we can believe that heaven exists with its own space and time. And because the spiritual energy of which heaven is created does not interact with the material energy of our physical world of the heavens and earth, there is no obvious contact between the two worlds—at least at the level of physical observation. Contacts are in the realm of the supernatural via the Holy Spirit. Nevertheless God, Creator and Sustainer of both worlds, wills that he be known and experienced in each one.[1]

The psalmist knew that there was no escape from the omnipresent God. "Where can I go from your Spirit? Where can I flee from your presence? If I go up to the heavens, you are there; if I make my bed in the depths, you are there. If I rise on the wings of the dawn, if I settle on the far side of the sea, even there your hand will guide me, your right hand will hold me fast . . ." (Ps. 139:7–10). And speaking through the prophet Amos, God himself declared: "Though they dig down to the depths of the grave, from there my hand will take them. Though they climb up to the heavens, from there I will bring them down . . ." (Am. 9:2ff.). Believers within the old covenant knew that the LORD is both with us and around us here on earth and far above and beyond us in heaven. He is able to be in the world, through the world and also above the world because he is the LORD, the self-existent Spirit.

Today in the Western world it is apparently possible to spend a whole life on earth without experiencing, or at least admitting to experiencing, the presence of God in and through the created order. This failure or omission is to be attributed to a combination of human sin and the secularism of society. One of the tasks of the churches in the West is to help people remove from their spiritual eyes the blindfolds of secularism in order that they can recognize the presence of God in his creation, of which they are a part.

One of the differences between being under the heavens and in heaven is that of the intensity of the experience of the presence and blessing of God. Heaven is a created sphere where God is known and experienced unmistakably as the God of grace and glory. He is manifest in at least three ways: first, by a more visible providence, making the whole order of things the evident expression of an infinite goodness; second, by a more abundant grace, making the minds of his people transparent to his thought and their hearts to his love; and third, by an incarnate presence with them in the glorified Man, Jesus Christ.[2] Even before the arrival of the Incarnate Word in the Ascension, the apprehension of the holy presence was both full and clear in heaven. This is apparent from the insights of the psalmist who, considering the heavenly host of angels who surrounded the LORD, exclaimed: "Who is like the LORD among the heavenly beings? In the council of the holy ones, God is greatly feared: he is more awesome than all who surround him" (Ps. 89:6–7). Here the fear of God is a profound reverence based on a sure and powerful sense of his holiness.

The Lord whom Isaiah saw in his vision in the Temple (Is. 6) and the Lord whom John saw in his vision on Patmos (Rev. 5; 7) are one and the same LORD, the self-existent Spirit, who eternally exists as Father, Son and Holy Spirit. The response to him by the angels whom Isaiah heard was a threefold one of "Holy, holy, holy is the LORD Almighty," and this was also heard by John (Rev. 4:8). However, John heard a further chorus of praise addressed "to the Lamb" and he saw the heavenly company bow down to worship the Lamb—the Incarnate Son. "To him who sits on the throne and to the Lamb be praise and honor and glory and power for ever and ever" (Rev. 5:13).

Heaven took on a new significance with the arrival of Jesus; the presence of the Lamb there created a new system of conditions within heaven, since created human nature now belonged personally to God, Creator and Redeemer. In entering space and time to become the Messiah, the eternal Son took to himself our human nature in the womb of the Virgin Mary. And when he rose from death to ascend into heaven, he did not leave behind his human body or nature. He took them in their transformed and spiritualized new existence into heaven. The result was that while God did not change he did gain an everlasting and permanent union with the created sphere we call heaven, since in heaven was, is and shall be the human nature of the eternal Son. Within heaven there is the permanent presence of the eternal Son not only in his deity and Godhead but also in his Manhood. God had acquired, as it were, a permanently everlasting human face, but without that human face ever being absorbed, negated or destroyed by deity. And it is because God has a human face that the pure in heart can see God: without their Mediator who is the Lamb, the pure in heart could never see God. They come to, and look upon, God as those united to him in and by his human nature, which they share.

In the New Testament, where there is the recognition and expression of God as Trinity, there is no systematic teaching concerning God as Three in One. We are presented with a series of dynamic images of Christ and the Spirit and their relation to the Father, together with occasional statements of a trinitarian character (e.g., the baptismal command of Matthew 28:19). The change in the nature of heaven is also highlighted through the use of images and the proclamation of various titles of the ascended Jesus. We must now look at some of these in order to gain scriptural insights into the nature of the heaven for which we ought to long.

1. *Sitting at the right hand of the Father.* In the first Christian sermon recorded in the Acts, Peter declares: "God has raised this Jesus to life, and we are all witnesses of the fact. Exalted to the right hand of God, he has received from the Father the promised Holy Spirit and has poured out what you now see and hear" (men speaking in languages they have never learnt as they praise God for the Resurrection of Jesus) (Acts 2:32, 33). Then he proceeded to quote from Psalm 110:1: "The LORD said to my Lord: sit at my right hand until I make your enemies a footstool for your feet." David is quoted as describing God speaking to the Messiah (his Lord) and telling him to sit at his right hand side while he overcomes all his enemies for him. Peter cited this Psalm because Jesus himself had used it to refer to himself in discussion with the Pharisees (Mk. 12:36).[3]

To sit at the right hand of the great and powerful king was to be in the position of the greatest honor, for it was to participate in the honor of the king himself. It was seen as the place of perfect happiness, of the exercise of authority and power, and of the closest possible relation to the king himself. By this image Peter and the other apostles highlighted the exaltation of Jesus to the highest place in heaven and to his sharing, as co-Regent, in the authority and rule of the Father. Further, they were suggesting that he could only sit in such a place because he was the Son who had an intimate relationship with the Father.

2. *Standing at the right hand of the Father.* Just before he was stoned to death to become the first Christian martyr, Stephen, full of the Holy Spirit, looked up to heaven and saw the glory of God, and Jesus standing at the right hand of God. "Look," he said, "I see heaven open and the Son of Man standing at the right hand of God" (Acts 7:55–56). Since Stephen gave to Jesus the title of Son of Man, we are reminded of Daniel's vision. He saw "one like a son of man, coming with the clouds of heaven. He approached the Ancient of Days and was led into his presence. He was given authority, glory and sovereign power; all peoples, nations and men of every language worshipped him . . ." (Dan. 7:13–14). Rejected by the Jewish leaders, Jesus is seen by Stephen as being crowned the King of kings and being given the authority and power of the Father. The fact that he is standing may suggest that as King and Judge he is ready to return to earth to exercise his authority as Judge and then inaugurate the kingdom of God of the age to come. Whatever the act of standing actually signifies, the place where he stands is the right hand; and thus this image again highlights the intimate relationship between the Father and the Incarnate Son in heaven.[4]

3. Interceding at the right hand of the Father. In explaining the wonderful position of believers who are united in and by the Spirit to their Lord in heaven, Paul described Jesus as being "at the right hand of God" and there "interceding for us" (Rom. 8:34)). The same image occurs in Hebrews 7:25. According to Paul, the Holy Spirit within our hearts intercedes for us—prays through us and on our behalf to God in heaven—and then the exalted Jesus, in the place of highest honor, completes the prayer by also interceding for us.

This is a strange picture. The One who is the co-Regent of the Father and who possesses full divine authority and power is presented as making requests on behalf of others to the Father. Of course, the picture is not of the Incarnate Son on bended knees imploring a reluctant heavenly Father to grant favors for those he does not wish to bless. It is of the crowned Son and Prince, who enjoys the total favor and intimacy of the Father, making requests on behalf of his friends, in whom already dwells the Holy Spirit, that they will always be recipients of the divine favor. Thus Jesus is presented as the Mediator and the One in, by, through and with whom we approach the Father.[5]

From these three images, we gain important insights into the nature of heaven—Christ Jesus is at its center, bringing the created to the Creator so that they become the new creation. Christ Jesus is the One by whom God relates to created beings and created beings relate to him; for them he is the Mediator, God and Man in one Person. These insights are confirmed when we examine that title which was quickly given to Jesus and which Paul especially much used—the title of Lord.

Kyrios, "Lord," was used in the Septuagint translation to render YHWH (Yahweh).[6] In the Roman Empire it was often used of the master and owner of slaves
as well as of the Emperor as Master of the empire. Paul
claimed that the Christian evangelists did not preach
about themselves but "Christ Jesus as Lord" (2 Cor.
4:5). He was their Master, and the universal Master,
appointed by God, and as such he demanded the obedience of faith and love. In the poem found in Philippians
2:6–11, the preexistence of the Son, his Incarnation, his
servanthood and suffering are affirmed; then the exaltation of Jesus to the highest place and with the greatest
name is celebrated; that name is what all will confess at
the End—"Jesus Christ is Lord." Thus the name of
"Lord" points to the possession of Godhead as well as
to the office of Jesus in heaven in his relation as Master
to believers and to the world as a whole.

It is also highly significant that throughout the recorded visions of John on Patmos the exalted Jesus is
called the Lamb. He who shares the Father's throne is
none other than he who was offered as a sacrificial lamb
on Mount Calvary for the sin of the world. He whom
the angels praise is he who has known to the full the
weight and burden of human sin and the wrath of God
against sin. And this same Incarnate Son is he in and
through whom the light and life of eternal life are
constantly and everlastingly supplied to the inhabitants
of heaven. In his description of the heavenly Jerusalem
(to which we shall return below), John tells that the
Lord God Almighty and the Lamb are its temple; further, the glory of God is its light and the Lamb is its
lamp. We may say that the future of heaven is the
future of the Lord Jesus Christ, the Lamb. Being

incorporated in Christ Jesus, we are not only incorporate with the Son of God, we are also incorporate with the Man who has reached the goal of creaturely existence.

While the change in the nature of heaven caused by God's exaltation of Jesus from the grave to heaven and his coronation there as Lord has been recognized by theologians, it is often overlooked in popular preaching, teaching and piety. This has not always been the case. The medieval Church redeveloped the doctrine of limbo, the limbo of infants and the limbo of the fathers of the old covenant.[7] The first was held to be for the souls of infants who died unbaptized and thereby lacked the grace of regeneration; the second was held to be for the souls of the faithful of the old covenant as they waited in relative contentment and happiness for the Messiah.

The *limbus patrum*, as it was called, was based on sound enough logic. Heaven, it was rightly said, is only heaven for forgiven and redeemed sinners when the Incarnate Son is there. But the Incarnate Son only arrived in heaven at his Ascension. Therefore, the faithful members of the old covenant could not, and did not, go to heaven when they died. Since God could not cast them into hell, and since they were the recipients of his gracious promises, he placed them in a temporary place and sphere, there to wait in natural, perfect happiness until the Incarnate Son came to lead them into heaven. Christ, it was said, visited these happy souls after his death on the Cross; he proclaimed to them his identity and then, at his Resurrection and Ascension, he led them into heaven to begin to enjoy to the full the vision of God and the attendant benefits and blessings.

We may not favor this doctrine today; and it is

certainly not a dogma of the Roman Catholic Church
(merely a theological opinion); however, the instincts
of those theologians who developed and taught it were
right. Heaven is not heaven for believers unless Jesus
Christ, in his Manhood and Godhead, is there. For, as
Revelation 21 and 22 make clear, the reality of knowing, loving, adoring and serving God, as God, in his
absolute Purity is only possible because in Christ there
is access to, and welcome from, this holy God. We have
claimed that heaven as a created sphere experienced a
profound and mighty change through the arrival and
coronation of Jesus, Messiah and Lord. Now we must
ask: Has heaven reached its final, completed and everlasting state, or will there be further changes or devel-
opments? The answer is that it has not yet reached its
ultimate state.

First of all, heavenly life is not static, fixed and
finalized: in heaven the saints are perfect, but perfect
only in potential, for they are in a process of moving
from glory into glory. God is inexhaustible in his holiness and in his love, and forever and forever they will
be growing into him through the Incarnate Son and by
the Holy Spirit. As the pure see God, they will be
supremely happy and yet become even more supremely
happy.

In the second place, heaven is continually expanding
in population through the arrival there of those who
have completed their earthly pilgrimage and service.
Certainly, they are there already in the sense that they
are there in Christ their Representative; but with their
physical deaths they are there in their own right as the
children of God in the house of their heavenly Father.

Thirdly, heaven will change at, and following, the

Parousia of Christ. Not only will heaven "descend" with Christ when the time arrives for the final judgment of the nations and people of the world, it will also become the only created sphere for the redeemed people of God. This claim requires further explanation. Heaven will descend with Christ, for he will bring the angels with him and he will also provide for the saints in heaven, as well as for the saints still on earth, resurrection bodies, like his own body. In those bodies the redeemed will be present at the final judgment to be vindicated by the grace of God at work in them. Further, at the close of the judgment this old world and age will cease to be; in the language of Isaiah (65:17) there will be new heavens and earth—a new created sphere. This created sphere, in which the redeemed will dwell as God's people in their resurrection bodies, is described in moving terms in Revelation:

> Then I saw a new heaven and a new earth, for the first heaven and the first earth had passed away, and there was no longer any sea. I saw the Holy City, the new Jerusalem, coming down out of heaven from God, prepared as a bride beautifully dressed for her husband. And I heard a loud voice from the throne saying, "Now the dwelling of God is with men, and he will live with them. They will be his people, and God himself will be with them and be their God. He will wipe every tear from their eyes. There will be no more death or mourning or crying or pain, for the old order of things has passed away" (21:1–4; see also 21:22–22:5).

In the new creation, which is the kingdom of God or heaven, there will be no barrier between one sphere of creation and another (as there is now between heaven and earth). In this entirely new order of existence, there will be perfect and loving communion with God through Christ and there will be the fullness of joy, peace and satisfaction. Potentiality will be always in the process of fulfillment and thus there will be no boredom or inertia. The inner perfection, unity and perfection of God who is Trinity will become that by, and towards which, his adopted children live.

It was because the early Christians so looked forward to the birth of the new age of the kingdom of God, when the division between earth and heaven would be done away, that they prayed that Aramaic prayer "*Maranatha*"—"Come Lord Jesus." Christ is now the Light of the world; in the new creation he will still be the Light. "I did not see a temple in the city, because the Lord God Almighty and the Lamb are its temple. The city does not need the sun or the moon to shine on it, for the glory of God gives it light and the Lamb is its lamp" (Rev. 21:22–23).

3. Treasure in Heaven

As believers, we read the teaching of Jesus concerning God's kingdom not merely as words uttered long ago but as living words spoken now by the exalted Lord Jesus in, through and by the Holy Spirit, to our hearts and minds. We know that these words were originally spoken in Aramaic to the disciples in ancient Palestine over a period of three years, that they were remembered by these disciples, were illuminated by the reality of the resurrected Jesus and the descent of the Holy Spirit within the disciples' minds, were translated into Greek, and were used by the apostles, evangelists and new churches before they were formally written down, eventually to appear as the Gospels we know and treasure.

Yet, since Jesus is the same yesterday, today and forever, we believe that his word of long ago is still God's word of revelation and instruction, salvation and redemption. Thus, when we read and consider the words of the historical Jesus, we do so not as historians or antiquaries but as those who are expecting to have a word from the living Lord Jesus in heaven. This approach does not set aside or neglect genuine biblical scholarship; it uses it in order to discover what the original words, recorded in the sacred text, meant, in order to clear the way for the Lord, by his Spirit, to show what they mean for today.

Our aim is to hear what the Lord Jesus has to say to us about longing for the heavenly realm in the context of communion and fellowship with God now.

In chapter 2 we observed how Jesus looked up and addressed God as " 'Abbā," thereby expressing his intimate communion with heaven and his sense of being one with God in holy love and divine purpose. Here we shall observe how Jesus drew his disciples into his relationship with the Father so that they, too, in dependence upon him, could begin to address God as " 'Abbā," and learn to trust and obey.

The Lord's Prayer

There are two versions of that prayer we call "the Lord's Prayer" in which disciples are taught to address God as " 'Abbā." The shorter version is found in Luke 11:2–4, provided by Jesus for disciples who wanted to know how to pray properly as his disciples. "Father, hallowed be your name, your kingdom come. Give us each day our daily bread. Forgive us our sins, for we also forgive everyone who sins against us. And lead us not into temptation."

The longer version is found in Matthew 6:9–13, provided by Jesus as an illustration of true prayer in comparison with certain contemporary Jewish forms of prayer. "Our Father in heaven, hallowed be your name, your kingdom come, your will be done on earth as it is in heaven. Give us today our daily bread. Forgive us our debts, as we also have forgiven our debtors. And lead us not into temptation, but deliver us from the evil one."

All the Lucan version is found in the Matthean version. What the latter has as extras are (a) a longer address to God as Father; (b) "your will be done . . ."; and (c) "but deliver us from the evil one." Jeremias has argued strongly that Jesus gave his disciples an Aramaic, not Hebrew, prayer, and that the Lucan form is nearest to the original. Thus the prayer begins with " '*Abbā*" (Greek: *patēr*.).[1]

By addressing God as " '*Abbā*," the disciples are given the great privilege of membership in the new covenant, the new Israel, the new creation, the new family of God of the kingdom of God of the age to come. They can address the Lord as if they were trusting and obedient children speaking to their caring and generous fathers. Barriers of sin and tradition are removed as they are given the privilege of being placed in a relationship with God of the same kind that Jesus himself enjoys. Their prayer is to be the verbal expression of a life of continuing communion with God as his will is done.

And being faithful and grateful children of God, disciples will desire to pray for the end of this age and the birth of the new age of the kingdom of God. This entails hallowing his name now through reverence and honor and through obedience to his commands. It also involves longing for the final establishment of God's gracious sovereignty with the arrival of the kingdom of peace, righteousness and fellowship. For us it involves longing for the Parousia of Jesus Christ—his second coming to judge the living and the dead.

Further, they will pray for daily bread. Much research has gone into the possible Aramaic background of this petition, and there seems to be a general agreement that what Jesus intended (and for us intends still) was "the bread of today and tomorrow," which is a comprehensive request both for the physical needs of today as well as for participation in the great feast of the kingdom of God of the age to come—the Messianic banquet (see Lk. 13:29; Mt. 8:11; Lk. 6:21; Mt. 5:6; Lk. 12:37; Mt. 25:1–13; Mt. 22:1–14; Lk. 14:16–24; 22:30). Again the prayer involves longing for the heavenly realm.

As they ask for God's forgiveness, which is like that of a loving earthly father towards his sincere child, disciples are to be always ready to forgive others; for where the readiness to forgive is absent, the request for forgiveness from heaven is a lie. Disciples are to reflect the quality of the kingdom of heaven in their behavior and attitudes. The final petition seems harsh and abrupt; this is because it refers to the last great trial before the arrival of the kingdom and is a prayer that within that time of trial they will not fall prey to temptation and fall away from their heavenly course.

Thus the Lord's Prayer is a prayer for those who are in communion with God, who are living in trust and obedience, who are longing for the arrival of the kingdom of God in its fullness, and who want to participate in the great time of the completion of salvation and redemption. For us today, it is a prayer for those who are conscious of their membership in the heavenly family of God and who long for the fullness of family life which will come with the Parousia of Christ, the resurrection of the dead, and the establishment of the full reality of the kingdom of God. As we shall see in the next chapter, it is also a prayer for those in whom dwells the Holy Spirit, the Spirit of sonship, in whom we cry " *'Abbā*, Father."

To see what this Prayer is all about is to be warned of its possible careless use in liturgy by reciting it merely in parrot fashion. It is to be said together by those who are consciously seeking to follow Jesus and for whom it is a privilege, which money cannot buy, to be able to call God " *'Abbā*."

Treasure in Heaven

In the Sermon on the Mount, Matthew includes not only a section on prayer, in which is the Lord's Prayer, but also teaching concerning treasure in heaven, singleness of mind, and seeking first the kingdom of God. Since these themes are integral to our concerns, we shall look at each one. Here is what Jesus said about treasures:

> Do not store up for yourselves treasures on earth, where moth and rust destroy, and where thieves break in and steal. But store up for yourselves treasures in heaven, where moth and rust do not destroy, and where thieves do not break in and steal. For where your treasure is, there your heart will be also (Mt. 6:19–21; cf. Lk. 12:33–34).[2]

In an oriental setting, that which people treasured included costly clothing, which was always liable to be attacked by moths and thus be rendered of no value. It also included a variety of metal objects which were always susceptible to rusting and thus losing their luster. (The word translated "rust" is *brosis* and refers to any act of corrosion or being eaten. Thus it may also refer to precious farm produce being devoured by vermin.) And, quite apart from the effects of corrosion and decay, there is always the possibility that one's precious possessions will be stolen by thieves.

Therefore, if a person allows his or her life to be governed by commitment to his or her cherished valuables, that person must not be surprised if the center of his or her life collapses through their corruption or loss. This is what we may call commonsense logic, which needs to be heard today as much as when it was first uttered by Jesus. While we have more sophisticated ways of preserving and guarding our precious possessions, the possibilities of our losing them have also increased as crime has become more sophisticated and as the value of money is so variable.

In contrast, treasure in heaven is absolutely safe; it is exempt from decay, corrosion or loss of value, since it is in a sphere where it is guaranteed by Almighty God himself!

But what is treasure in heaven? We must not assume that it refers to some special reward which already preexists. It refers to God himself. At the end of the parable of the rich fool (Lk. 12:13–21) who amasses possessions, only to die before he can enjoy them, Jesus comments: "This is how it will be with anyone who stores up things for himself but is not rich towards God." Having treasure in heaven is being rich towards God; it is also having eternal life, enjoying now a taste of the life of the kingdom to come, and thus longing for its fullness in that kingdom. This meaning comes out in the conversation between the young man and Jesus which is recorded by all three synoptic Gospels. Jesus told this rich young Jew that if he wanted eternal life and God's salvation, he had to sell his possessions (which he dearly loved), give to the poor and join the band of disciples. When he did this, said Jesus, he would have "treasure in heaven" (Mt. 19:21; Mk. 10:21; Lk. 18:22). The treasure is a relationship with God which includes the gift of eternal life, the privilege of communion with him and calling him " '*Abbā*," and of knowing that one's future is totally secure in his keeping. We read and hear these words about "treasure in heaven" knowing the Lord Jesus is exalted and seated at the right hand of the Father. Thus, for us, treasure in heaven is defined with reference to Jesus, in, through and with whom is our treasure.

Here is what Jesus said about singleness of mind:

> The eye is the lamp of the body. If your eyes are good, your whole body will be full of light. But if your eyes are bad, your whole body will be full of darkness. If then the light within you is darkness, how great is that darkness!
>
> No one can serve two masters. Either he will hate the one and love the other, or he will be devoted to the one and despise the other. You cannot serve God and Money. (Mt. 6:22–24; cf. Lk. 11:34–36; 16:13)

The "eye" here points to the total orientation and direction of a person's life. The word translated "good" is *haplous*, referring to health and thus to undivided loyalty and commitment to that which gives health. Again Jesus is teaching that true health and wholeness of life are gained when the spiritual and moral eyes are focused upon God, his will and word. And this again for us means looking to the exalted Jesus as both our Lifegiver and Lord, and not allowing anything to come between him and us.

The fact that one cannot serve faithfully two masters, especially when each one has totally different demands, is part of the logic of common sense, easier recognized than practiced. The word translated "money" is "*mamōnas*," which can mean money or wealth. It is well known that the love of (that is, the service of) money is a root of all kinds of evil (1 Tim. 6:10). In the affluence of the West, with the abundance of consumer goods available and advertisers' pressures to get them and keep up with the neighbors, it is so easy to seek to serve two masters—God in Christ and the secularist spirit of the age. Disciples are called to have single-minded commitment to their Master, into whose presence they look forward to entering.

And, finally, here is what Jesus said about seeking God's kingdom:

> Do not worry, saying, "What shall we eat?" or "What shall we drink?" or "What shall we wear?" For the pagans run after all these things, and your heavenly Father knows that you need them. But seek first his kingdom and his righteousness, and all these things shall be given to you as well (Mt. 6:31–33; cf. Lk. 12:31).

To appreciate the full force of the words of Jesus, the whole section, verses 25 to 34, should be read (cf. Lk. 12:22–31). The emphasis is on exclusive commitment to God and his will; and since God is Creator and Lord, he will supply the temporal and transient needs of his children. God's kingdom is his gracious and sovereign rule as Father; this begins in individual hearts and lives, is to be manifested in the community experience and fellowship of these who call him " '*Abbā*," and will be fully expressed in the life of the world to come. Righteousness points to right relationships between forgiven

sinners and their heavenly Father and among the forgiven sinners themselves.

In the West today, there is no basic shortage of food
or clothing, but the problem for many is which food to
choose and what brand or style of clothing to wear!
This causes anxiety just as much as does the problem to
which Jesus referred—which is still a problem for many
in our world. To seek first God's kingdom today is to be
dedicated to the One who is the King of that kingdom,
even the exalted and crowned Lord Jesus Christ. To
seek righteousness is to desire to be in right relationships with heaven and with fellow human beings on
earth.[3] And neither of these can be sought apart from
the internal desire to complete the will of God on earth
and be prompted to the richer fellowship in heaven.

Fellowship in Heaven

Jesus spoke often of the future coming of the Son of
Man to earth in order to execute God's judgment in
justifying the righteous and condemning the wicked.
Most of what he had to say is in the highly symbolic
language of apocalyptic literature which had been much
used within Judaism for a couple of centuries or more.
Intermingled with his prophecies of the future coming
of the Son of Man are prophecies concerning the fall of
Jerusalem (which happened in A.D. 70).[4]

At the end of one of those prophecies Jesus told the
disciples:

No one knows about that day or hour, not even the angels in
heaven, nor the Son, but only the Father. Be on guard! Be
alert! You do not know when that time will come. It's like a

man going away: he leaves his house in charge of his servants, each with his assigned task, and tells the one at the
door to keep watch.

Therefore keep watch because you do not know when the
owner of the house will come back—whether in the evening,
or at midnight or when the cock crows, or at dawn. If he
comes suddenly, do not let him find you sleeping. What I
say to you, I say to everyone. "Watch" (Mk. 13:32–37; cf.
Mt. 25:14–15b; 24:42; 25:13; Lk. 19:12–13).

Longing for the heavenly realm means longing to be
with Christ; thus it includes longing for his return to
earth to consummate the purpose of God in this age.

Concerning his return, disciples are to "be on guard,
be alert, and be watching"—which is the opposite of
sleeping and having no interest or care. Yet this does
not mean that the disciple will not be engaged in work.
As the parable makes clear, the way to be vigilant is not
to be permanently looking for the arrival of the Master
and thereby doing no work; rather, it is to be doing the
kind of work which the Master has commanded and
approves at the same time as longing and praying for
his return. Each disciple has his work from the Master,
and by completing it in the right spirit, he is effectively
being alert and watching. Of course, that "work" includes time for worship, prayer and meditation as well
as the more practical activity of loving the neighbor in a
variety of ways. When this relationship of work and
watching is recognized, then it can be seen that only
those who are genuinely heavenly minded can be of
earthly use in the will and purpose of God. Those who
desire the Master's return, and/or their call to be with
him in heaven before his return, will be his genuine
and effective servants on earth, for they will truly be
alert and vigilant.

Not only did Jesus command his disciples to watch, he also promised that they would experience super-abundant fellowship and joy in the kingdom of God of the new age and creation, following the general resurrection and final judgment.[5] He therefore encouraged them to look forward to the joy of that age as he made use of the traditional image of the great banquet, much favored by Jewish writers and rabbis. Isaiah had described the future gracious and universal reign of the Lord in this manner: "On this mountain the Lord Almighty will prepare a feast of rich food for all peoples, a banquet of aged wine—the best of meats and the finest of wines" (Is. 25:6). And Jesus declared: "I say to you that many will come from the east and the west and will take their places at the feast with Abraham, Isaac and Jacob in the kingdom of heaven" (Mt. 8:11; cf. Lk. 13:29). The same important theme is illustrated in his parable of the wedding banquet, which begins: "The kingdom of heaven is like a king who prepared a wedding banquet . . ." (Mt. 22:1–14; cf. Lk. 14:16–24).

Luke combined teaching by Jesus concerning watchfulness with participation in the fellowship of the great feast: "It will be good for those servants whose master finds them watching when he comes. I tell you the truth, he will dress himself to serve, will have them recline at the table and will come and wait on them" (Lk. 12:37). Here the roles of master and servants are reversed. The master prepares a real feast and himself serves his servants as they recline at his table. Thus it shall be in the age to come that Christ will personally wholly meet the needs of his disciples, who will be the recipients both of his grace and of the joy of the fellowship of the new people of God.

Three Gospels in their account of the Last Supper

include words of Jesus concerning the fellowship, joy and feasting of the kingdom of God which shall surely come in its fullness: "I tell you the truth. I will not drink again of the fruit of the vine until that day when I drink it anew in the kingdom of God" (Mk. 14:25, cf. Mt. 26:29; Lk. 22:18). "That day" points to the Parousia of the Son of Man, which is to be followed by the creation of perfect and continual fellowship between God in Christ and his covenant people as they enjoy the salvation and new creation which Christ has gained for them. (The cup which Jesus did not drink was probably the fourth cup used in the Passover ritual; to it was tied the promise that God will take his people to be with him forever; Ex. 6:6–7.)

Thus the kingdom to which disciples are to look forward will include fellowship and joy of a superabundant and amazing quality. It will also be for them a sphere of enlarged opportunity to serve their Lord and Savior. This is to be deduced from the parables of Jesus in which servants are placed in charge of more lands or given added and further responsibilities because of their faithfulness (see Lk. 12:44; Mt. 24:47; Lk. 19:17, 19). Then, also, life in the kingdom will be so different from what disciples know on this earth in the present age that the only word to describe it is "new." There will be a renewal of all things at or after the Parousia, said Jesus (Mt. 19:28), and the promise of the Lord in Isaiah 43:19 will be fulfilled: "See, I am doing a new thing!"

One illustration of this new creation relates to marriage. The common Jewish expectation was that earthly relationships in a deeper and purer form would be resumed after the Resurrection. But Jesus said: "When the dead rise, they will neither marry nor be given in marriage; they will be like the angels in heaven" (Mk.

12:25; Mt. 22:30; Lk. 20:34–36). Because it will be *new*, Jesus provided few concrete details, leaving his disciples fully to experience the new quality of life when they actually arrived in the kingdom! However, in the present age they experienced the new life, power and peace in the presence and activity of Jesus, the Messiah, and then, after his Ascension, in the presence and activity of the Holy Spirit.

Of the future kingdom, Jesus spoke of it as "blessed," meaning truly happy.[6] After the final judgment of the nations, the Son of Man will say to those on his right side: "Come, you who are blessed by my Father; take your inheritance, the kingdom prepared for you since the creation of the world" (Mt. 25:34). In both Hebrew and Greek there are two words usually translated as "blessed." In the Hebrew Old Testament the word *baruk* is normally applied only to God (e.g., Ps. 28:6), while the second, *ashrey*, is usually used of man (e.g., Ps. 1:1). The comparative Greek words are *eulogētos* and *makarios*. In the text just quoted, *eulogemonos* (a cognate of *eulogetēs*) is used so that the righteous are virtually called "the blessed of the Blest One, the Father." In contrast, the word used in the beatitudes is *makarios*, which means truly happy and is used as the opposite of woe (Mt. 5:3–12; cf. Lk. 6:20–23).

Each beatitude contains one part of the truth about life in the kingdom of God. As a ray of light passes through a prism to be broken up into the colors of the rainbow, so the reality of the kingdom for the faithful is expressed in the colorful promises of the beatitudes. What it means to be "the blest of the Blessed" is contained in the second half of each beatitude. Thus Jesus was saying something like this: "Oh, the genuine happiness [*makarios*] of the blessed [*eulogetēs*]." The latter is then expressed in terms of possessing the kingdom, being comforted, inheriting the earth, being satisfied, obtaining mercy, seeing God and being called the children of God. And while these gifts and privileges are experienced in part in this life, they belong in their fullness to the age to come and are thus what genuine disciples long for.

Eternal Life

In his Prologue, John told his readers that in the Word "was life and that life was the light of men"[7] (Jn. 1:4). Life (zoē) and light (phōs) go together; he who has life is the Revealer of deity. The Word made flesh, the Son and the Messiah, is the life (11:25; 14:6), the bread of life (6:35, 48), the light of life (8:12), who gives the water of life (4:10ff.; 7:38) and bread of life (6:50ff.). His words are spirit and life (6:63) and actual words of eternal life (6:68). And this life (zoē) cannot be put to death, for when Jesus dies upon the Cross, it is his mortal life (psychē) which he gives up in death.

To receive the Incarnate Son and to believe in him result in the bestowal of revelation and of eternal life (3:16). It is noteworthy that eternal life is first mentioned in the Gospel immediately after the sole reference to the kingdom of God (3:3, 5). Thus the Johannine emphasis upon eternal life as the gift of God received in this age in anticipation of its fullness in the age to come resembles the emphasis in the Synoptics upon God's saving rule coming into human lives now. In fact, a study of the seventeen references to eternal life show that while reference to the age to come is retained, it is not prominent (3:15; 3:16; 3:36; 4:14; 4:36; 5:24;

5:39; 6:27; 6:40; 6:47; 6:54; 6:68; 10:28; 12:25; 12:50; 17:2; 17:3). Eternal life is presented as a quality and depth of life given by God to believers in this age in order that they might genuinely know him in this age and more profoundly and satisfyingly in the age to come.

The function of "eternal" (*aiōnios*), which literally means "pertaining to an age," is to give a quantitative definition to the qualitative life, received as God's gift. It is the life of the age that begins after the Last Judgment and which has no end. And that which is properly a future blessing becomes a present fact in virtue of the realization of the future in Jesus, the Messiah. The possession of the gift of eternal life through belief in the Messiah in this age as an anticipation of its full possession in the age to come is a theme much emphasized in John's Gospel. In this "spiritual" Gospel eternal life is always presented as the gift of God to the believer: neither the Father nor the Son is said to have it, since the Father "has life in himself" (5:26) and he has granted this same life to the Son (5:26).

The truth that eternal life is received in the present is clear from such a statement of Jesus' as this: "I tell you the truth, whoever hears my word and believes him who sent me has eternal life and will not be condemned; he has crossed over from death to life" (5:24). However, the future gaining of life is made clear in this promise, made to the Samaritan woman at the well: "Whoever drinks the water I give him will never thirst. Indeed the water I give him will become in him a spring of water welling up to eternal life" (4:14; see also 4:36; 5:28; 6:27; 12:25).

If the primary characteristic of the possession of eternal life now is genuine knowledge of God and communion with him in the life of faith and faithfulness, then to what do the believing faithful look forward? In his priestly prayer, recorded in John 17, Jesus prayed: "Father, I want those you have given me to be with me where I am, and to see my glory, the glory you have given me because you loved me before the creation of the world" (v. 24). To be present with Christ and to have fellowship with him in the sphere of his glorified Being constitute a much deeper and more profound experience of grace than the highest moments of spiritual fellowship on earth in this age. The glory of the exalted Jesus is the radiance of his eternal deity, which he shares with the Father in the unity of the Holy Trinity. The final wish of Jesus was that his disciples be with him in his true home, the Father's presence; there they will "see his glory," not with human physical eyes but with the eyes of the heart and understanding, and thus be lost in wonder, love and praise.

In the Old Testament, glory refers not to God in his essential nature but to God in self-unveiling and self-revelation, especially in his mighty acts of salvation (Ex. 14:17ff.; Ps. 96:3). Because Jesus is the Incarnate Son of God, he radiates God's glory but does so in such a way that his followers (with whom he shares human nature) are enabled by grace to enjoy the power and blessing of the self-unveiling of God in and through him. Eternal life, a present possession, will be a future reality also, and will include being with Jesus forever and seeing the glory of God in him.

4. Patient Hope

When you look through the lists of the books of the New Testament, you quickly realize that half of them were written by the apostle Paul. His conversion from Pharisaic Judaism to Christianity occurred when he had a powerful vision of the exalted Lord Jesus, whom he saw as gloriously alive and not dead. From this moment until his martyrdom in Rome, Paul served his Master as the apostle to the non-Jews (Gentiles). His whole ministry was based on his experience of the living, ruling Christ, and upon his conviction that his Master is enthroned in heaven at the right hand of the Father. He was supremely conscious of being united with his heavenly Lord in and by the Holy Spirit, who guided him in his apostolic labors. Thus he wrote warmly of being an adopted child of God, of enjoying union with the Lord Jesus and of being led by the Spirit in his journey to his heavenly Lord and in his life in and with him. Paul was spiritually minded, which is another way

of saying that he was heavenly minded, and this possession of the mind of Christ, far from making him of
little earthly use, actually gave his apostolic work a
special energy and direction.

In this chapter we shall note he taught that believers
are the adopted children of God and thus in enjoyment
of communion with heaven, that believers are part of
the new creation that God is making in heaven centered
upon the Lord Jesus, and, in greater detail, how the
Christian life is characterized by hope, itself fed by faith
and love. Hope for Paul is not some general uncertain
expectation of future happiness; it is an earnest expectation, proceeding from faith, trust and confidence in
God and his word, and accompanied by longing desires of enjoyment and fulfillment, of life in and with
Christ in love, worship and service of the Father in
heaven.

In Christ We Are God's Children

God is addressed as Father on forty occasions in the
Letters of Paul. Several times he opens his epistles with
the expression "Grace and peace to you from God our
Father . . ." (Rom. 1:7; 1 Cor. 1:3; Eph. 1:2; Col.
1:2). And at times he broke into praise of the Father—
"Praise be to the God and Father of our Lord Jesus
Christ, the Father of compassion and the God of all
comfort, who comforts us in all our troubles" (2 Cor.
1:3; see also Eph. 1:3). Like his Master, Paul carefully
distinguished between the relation of Jesus to the Father and the relation of disciples of Jesus to the Father.
Believing sinners became the *adopted*, not natural, sons

of God the Father. Further, in two of his Letters, Paul retains the Aramaic word, *'Abbā*, as he describes the intimate communion and fellowship between the faithful disciple and his Father in heaven.

To the churches of Galatia he writes: "When the time had fully come, God sent his Son, born of a woman, born under law, to redeem those under law, that we might receive the full rights of sons. Because you are sons, God sent the Spirit of his Son into our hearts, the Spirit who calls out ' *'Abbā*, Father' " (Gal. 4:4–6). Here we have the Incarnation of the eternal Son, who, as Man, becomes our Redeemer in order that we might be made members of the family of God himself and enjoy intimate communion as we call him "Father." In fact, this is made possible because, following the ascent of the Incarnate Son, there followed the descent of the Spirit (sent by the Father in the name of the Son) not only to cause the new birth but also to dwell within the heart of each faithful believer. And dwelling in each heart and speaking on behalf of the exalted Son, the Spirit causes or helps the genuine Christian to experience an intimate relationship with the Father, through the Son, and cry out " *'Abbā*."

Then, also, in addressing the believers in Rome, Paul writes: "For you did not receive a Spirit that makes you a slave again to fear, but you received the Spirit of sonship. And by him we cry, ' *'Abbā*, Father.' The Spirit himself testifies with our spirit that we are God's children" (Rom. 8:15, 16). Paul is probably looking back to their conversion and baptism to remind them of the great inheritance into which they entered by their incorporation into Christ. God the Father has adopted them as his children, and in sending the Holy Spirit (the Spirit of Christ) into their hearts, he has given them the Spirit of sonship and thereby provided the internal assurance of their communion with him. It is possible that Paul is also thinking of the use of the Lord's Prayer in the young churches, where it is probable that the Aramaic word 'Abbā was retained to address God as Father.

So we see continuity between the practice and teaching of Jesus and the teaching of Paul, the apostle to the Gentiles, who experienced God as 'Abbā. What is different is that with the exaltation of Jesus, the Spirit, who rested on him and worked in and through him when he was on earth, is now given to each believer in order to live within his or her soul and bring him or her the spiritual and moral assurance and conviction of being a child—an adopted child—of God. Thus an inner experience is married to a firm trust in God and his promises of grace and salvation.[1]

According to Paul, Christ forms such a unity with those who believe in him that it can be said that they are "in him." "If anyone is in Christ he is a new creation: the old has gone and the new has come" (2 Cor. 5:17). In fact, Paul often speaks of being crucified, dead, buried and raised with Christ (Rom, 6:3ff.; Gal. 2:19; Col. 2:12–13; 20; 3:1–3) and also of being made to sit with him in heaven (Eph. 2:6) and of appearing with him in glory (Col. 3:4). The apostle believes that the relationship of Christ to his people, the Church of God, is like that of the first man, Adam, to the human race. Adam was an individual person, but he was also a federal or representative person, for everything he did in terms of his relationship to God he did, as it were, for all his physical descendants. Thus

Adam sinned and through that sin all people became sinners. Jesus of Nazareth was an individual person, but he was also (and of course remains) a federal or representative person. As such, what he did he did on behalf of those whom he represented and for whom he substituted.

Paul, when explaining the symbolism of baptism by immersion in water, teaches that in this sacrament the convert and new believer is identified with Christ in death, burial and resurrection to new life (Rom. 6:3ff.). His true position is that he is a new creation in that he has put away sin, risen to new life and has entered into the joys of the heavenly realm: this is because he has entered into Christ, that is, into the body of Christ, and thus to him is counted that which Christ, his Head, has in store for him as a believer. However, in the day-to-day reality of living in the old world and evil age, he knows that he has not yet attained in daily experience that which he possesses in the exalted Christ. His aim must be to seek to live each day as one who belongs to Christ and to the heavenly realm.[2]

It is not, therefore, surprising to find that Paul refers to the grace of God which is freely given to believing sinners in three tenses. He explains that we have been saved by the death and resurrection of Jesus, that we are in the process of being saved through the work of the Holy Spirit in our lives, and that we shall be saved when, clothed in new resurrection bodies, we enter into the fullness of life in the kingdom of God (Eph. 2:5–8; 1 Cor. 1:18; Rom, 5:10). Thus salvation is past, present and future; what we have in Christ and are experiencing in the Spirit, we are eagerly to look forward to possessing in fullness.[3] The same holds true of righteousness and justification. By faith and through the death and resurrection of Jesus Christ, we are justified—a completed act; by the ministry of the Holy Spirit in our hearts, we are being made righteous; and in the new age of the kingdom of God, we shall not only be declared but in practice be judged righteous before God (Rom. 8:30; 6:13ff.; Gal. 5:5).[4] And, we may note, the same also holds true of sanctification.[5] By the death and resurrection of Christ, we have been set apart from sin for the service of God; by the ministry of the Holy Spirit, we are being set free from sin and its power and liberated to serve God joyfully; and finally, when we receive our resurrection bodies, we shall be wholly set apart for the worship and service of God (1 Cor. 1:2, 30; 1 Th. 4:3; Rom. 6:19–22).

Thus faith, hope and love belong intimately together for by faith we accept and appropriate the promises of God concerning Christ; by God's love we seek to live as those being saved, made righteous and being sanctified, knowing that love is the fulfillment of God's law; and in hope we patiently wait for the fulfillment of the promises of God in the kingdom of heaven, when love will be supreme. Here we shall focus our primary attention on hope, which we must look at first in general terms and then via specific texts.

"Christ in You, the Hope of Glory"

The main emphasis on hope in the New Testament is in the Letters of Paul: there nineteen out of thirty-one occurrences of the verb and thirty-six out of fifty-three occurrences of the noun within the whole New Testa-

ment are found. It is the apostle who fills out the
testimony of the Old Testament which speaks of "to
hope in the LORD" and "to wait for the LORD."
Jeremiah addressed God as "O Hope of Israel" (Jer.
14:8; 17:13), and the psalmist confessed: "In your
name I will hope" (Ps. 52:9). These men recognized
that hope was a gift from God founded upon his character and their covenant relationship with him. This also
Paul fully accepts as he prays for the church in Rome in
these words: "May the God of hope fill you with all joy
and peace as you trust in him, so that you may overflow with hope by the power of the Holy Spirit" (Rom.
15:13; cf. 2 Th. 2:16). Yet Paul, with all the apostles,
knows that with the advent of Christ there had also
come a fundamental change in the content of hope in
God. Now it must be confessed that "Christ Jesus is our
hope" (1 Tim. 1:1; cf. Col. 1:27). What is looked for
and awaited in the future is defined with reference to
the One who has come to reveal God to us. It is not a
vague hope, since the identity of Christ and what he
has done for sinners is already known.[6]

Hope is a patient, disciplined and humbly confident
waiting for, and eager expectation of, the Parousia of
the Lord Jesus. It includes that which Jesus conveyed by
his call "to watch and pray" and may be characterized
as movement towards a goal through trial and tribulation and disciplined waiting. The goal is full salvation (1
Th. 5:8), complete righteousness (Gal. 5:5), eternal life
(Tit. 1:2; 3:7) and an immortal resurrection body in
the glory of God (Rom 5:2; Col. 1:27; 2 Cor. 3:12).
Those who have this hope, Paul teaches, are willing and
ready to make sacrifices in order to gain its fulfillment.
Referring to the training of an athlete he says: "Every-

one who competes in the games goes into strict training. They do it to get a crown that will not last; but we
do it to get a crown that will last for ever" (1 Cor.
9:25).

Romans

In the Letter to the Romans. Paul uses the word *elpis*
("hope") on thirteen occasions.[7] For example, he writes:
"We rejoice in the hope of the glory of God. Not only
so, but we also rejoice in our sufferings, because we
know that suffering produces perseverance; perseverance, character; and character, hope. And hope does not
disappoint us, because God has poured out his love into
our hearts by the Holy Spirit whom he has given us"
(5:2–5). Here hope is linked with rejoicing in expectation of what shall be, with patient endurance in suffering and with the love of God. It is the goal of the
kingdom, to which hope points and moves, that gives
the reason and the strength to rejoice and to persevere.
In fact, the paragraph from which these verses are taken
shows clearly that the triad of faith, hope and love
belongs together for Christianity in this age and that
there cannot be genuine faith and love where there is
not hope as well.

Then, in chapter 8, Paul writes: "We know that the
whole creation has been groaning as in the pains of
childbirth right up to the present time. Not only so, but
we ourselves, who have the first fruits of the Spirit,
groan inwardly as we wait eagerly for our adoption as
sons, the redemption of our bodies. For in this hope we
were saved. But hope that is seen is no hope at all.

Who hopes for what he already has? But if we hope for what we do not yet have, we wait for it patiently" (8:22–25). Here Paul refers to the belief commonly held in Judaism that the age of the Messiah and/or the age of the kingdom of God will only appear after a time of upheaval and pain. He pictures this present world and age as a pregnant woman in labor preparing to give birth to the new world and new age of God's peace and righteousness.

Within this world are God's regenerate people in whom is the Spirit; by this Spirit these believers have a foretaste of the coming kingdom, and they both groan and eagerly await the arrival of that kingdom, when they will be given new, immortal resurrection bodies of glory. Since they have only a taste of the future, they hope for the fullness of salvation in the future.

Hope is thus an integral part of the Christian life, since it is produced by the indwelling Spirit, and it orientates the heart and life toward Christ, who is exalted in heaven, there preparing to return to consummate God's purposes on earth. Christianity without hope is like a car without headlamps.

2 Corinthians

In 1 Corinthians 4:16 to 5:10, Paul has much to say about the Christian hope, but he does not actually use the word "hope."[8] We shall look at this passage in three parts. First, 4:16–18:

Therefore we do not lose heart. Though outwardly we are wasting away, yet inwardly we are being renewed day by day. For our light and momentary troubles are achieving for us an eternal glory that far outweighs them all. So we fix our eyes not on what is seen, but on what is unseen. For what is seen is temporary, but what is unseen is eternal.

Earlier, Paul had been describing the hardships, difficulties and tribulations faced by apostles and evangelists as they worked for Christ in the Roman Empire. Within these trials they had experienced the grace of God through the presence and power of the indwelling Spirit. Thus they did not lose heart, and though their bodies showed signs of their maltreatment, they knew the power of God in their souls. They were confident that in serving Christ and doing the will of God they were living in genuine hope, truly watching and being alert and ready to meet their Lord when he came in glory.

They did not take their aims and objectives from that which they could see within the Roman Empire or within Judaism. They looked up in faith to the exalted Lord and hoped for his Parousia, setting their aim and purpose by him and his revealed will. It is always easier to believe that what is seen is more important than what cannot be seen—and this is particularly so in our generation today in the West. The heavenly realm is, however, invisible and is only encountered in the Holy Spirit through the triad of faith, hope and love.

Secondly, 5:1–5:

Now we know that if the earthly tent we live in is destroyed, we have a building from God, an eternal house in heaven, not built by human hands. Meanwhile we groan, longing to be clothed with our heavenly dwelling, because when we are clothed, we will not be found naked. For while we are in this tent, we groan and are burdened, because we do not wish to be unclothed but to be clothed with our heavenly dwelling, so that what is mortal may be swallowed up by life. Now it is God who has made us for this very purpose and has given us the Spirit as a deposit, guaranteeing what is to come.

Paul is so confident that believers will receive a new body, an immortal, spiritual body of glory, that he states that we already have such a body waiting, as it were, for us in and with the exalted Christ.

The presence of the Holy Spirit in our hearts causes us to long to be in that body and thus released from the present body of sin and decay. In fact, the presence of the indwelling Spirit within our souls in this mortal body is itself the guarantee of the reception in the age to come of a new body, which will be wholly indwelt and guided by the Holy Spirit, who is the Spirit of Christ. By his statement "we will not be found naked" Paul appears to suggest that when a Christian dies he appears as a naked spirit before Christ until the time of the Parousia, when he will gain his resurrection body. Thus Paul prefers not to die and be a naked spirit but to be alive and be changed at the Parousia. But whatever precisely Paul believed about the state of the Christian dead before the Parousia, there is no escaping from his confession of "longing to be clothed with our heavenly dwelling," be that at death or at the Parousia.

Thirdly, 5:6–10:

Therefore we are always confident and know that as long as we are at home in the body we are away from the Lord. We live by faith, not by sight. We are confident, I say, and would prefer to be away from the body and at home with the Lord. So we make it our goal to please him, whether we are at home in the body or away from it. For we must all appear before the judgment seat of Christ, that each one may receive what is due to him for the things done while in the body, whether good or bad.

The true home of a Christian is in the heavenly realm with Christ and in a body of immortality and glory. The faithful Christian always longs to be at home; however, while he is still in his mortal body and on earth, his one aim is to please his Lord by doing his will and hoping for eternal glory. There is no place whatever for idleness, laziness or inactivity in the Christian life, because each of us must appear before Christ to give an account of how thoroughly we lived in authentic faith, hope and love. Again we see that genuine heavenly-mindedness is productive of doing the will of God and good works.

Philippians

The letter to the church in Philippi is permeated with the notes of joy and of hope in Christ.[9] Paul tells the faithful there:

> I will continue to rejoice, for I know that through your prayers and the help given me by the Spirit of Jesus Christ, what has happened to me will turn out for my deliverance. I eagerly expect and hope that I will in no way be ashamed, but will have sufficient courage so that now as always Christ will be exalted in my body whether by life or by death. For to me, to live is Christ and to die is gain. If I am to go on living in the body, this will mean fruitful labor for me. Yet what shall I choose? I do not know! I am torn between the

two; I desire to depart and be with Christ, which is better by far; but it is more necessary for you that I remain in the body. Convinced of this, I know that I will remain, and I will continue with all of you for your progress and joy in the faith, so that through my being with you again, your joy in Christ Jesus will overflow on account of me (1:18b–26).

Paul wrote this while a prisoner of the Roman authorities. He is humbly confident that whether or not he will be acquitted in a Roman court, his stand for Christ will be vindicated, for inside and outside of the court he will proclaim Christ. His eager expectation is a state of enthusiastic anticipation of the future, the craning of the neck, as it were, to catch a glimpse of what lies ahead. He possesses a concentrated and intensely dynamic hope which ignores what looms in the immediate present and future as it stretches forward to embrace the true and real future, God's future. To face the immediate future he prays for courage and boldness in speaking of Christ, even if that means a certain death.

In contemplating both his death and his deliverance, Paul expresses the content of his Christian hope as well as his dedication to the task of apostle to the Gentiles. For him, living is living for Christ, and dying is dying into Christ. At a purely personal level of attaining salvation, the departing to be with Christ is preferable, for he will enjoy a richer and closer fellowship with his Lord; but at the level of the needs of the world, remaining in the world to work as an apostle is to be preferred, for by this means the Church will be edified and extended. It seems that the needs of his converts weighed heavier in his moral judgment than his own attainment of full salvation, and this is expressed in the last sentence.

Later, Paul writes these words as he encourages his converts to imitate the way that he believed, trusted and lived: "Our commonwealth is in heaven and from it we await a Savior, the Lord Jesus Christ, who will change our lowly body to be like his glorious body, by the power which enables him even to subject all things to himself. Therefore, my brethren, whom I love and long for, my joy and crown, stand firm thus in the Lord, my beloved" (3:20–4:1. RSV).

The word translated "commonwealth" is *politeuma* and can also be translated as "citizenship" (NIV). The word "commonwealth" is to be preferred because it carries the idea of the seat of government and thus points to heaven, where Christ is co-Regent with the Father, as the realm to which we belong and from where we are governed and ruled. Thus we have our true home and government in heaven, and on earth we are a colony of heaven's citizens, never forgetting our true home. Christians are as resident aliens on earth who belong to the commonwealth of heaven. As a colony of aliens we look and hope for the coming of our King in his glorious Parousia, when we shall be given bodies like his marvelous resurrection body.

In the light of such a prospect and hope, Paul encourages the church members to imitate him and his colleagues and thus to be fortified against false teachers and powerful temptations. Such is his concern for them that he calls them his "brethren," "joy," "crown" and "beloved"—all in one sentence.

Before he writes these lines in chapter 3 about the heavenly commonwealth, Paul had written in an intensely personal way: "I want to know Christ and the power of his resurrection and the fellowship of sharing in his sufferings, becoming like him in his death, and so, somehow, to attain to the resurrection from the dead" (3:10–11). Again Paul is recalling the symbolism of baptism, in which he died with Christ, and expressing his fervent desire that the life he lives will be an expression of the new life he has received from the resurrected Lord. Fully recognizing that what he is in Christ he has yet to attain within himself, Paul expresses his spiritual longing in these words: "I press on towards the goal to win the prize for which God has called me heavenwards in Christ Jesus" (v. 14), adding that "all of us who are mature should take such a view of things." The goal refers to the finishing post in a race, and thus Paul expresses his commitment to life as a race towards heaven, where is the crown of eternal life. Thus the Christian is not to see life as moving along a horizontal plane but as an upward climb or run towards Christ, who is in heaven. Unless there is such a goal, the accepting of discipline, privation and suffering makes no sense. Joy is only known through trials and difficulties when life is an upward run towards heaven.

Colossians[10]

In the first chapter, we read of "the faith and love that spring from the hope that is stored up for you in heaven" (v. 5). Here again we meet the triad of faith, hope and love and note how they belong to each other in the Christian life in this age and world. In Colossae were false teachers who were insisting that the future dimension of salvation was overemphasized; against them Paul reiterates the fullness of the Christian hope, which is in, with and through the exalted Christ, who is in heaven.

At the beginning of the third chapter, Paul develops this hope stored up in heaven in this way:

> Since, then, you have been raised with Christ, set your hearts on things above, where Christ is seated at the right hand of God. Set your minds on things above, not on earthly things. For you died, and your life is now hidden with Christ in God. When Christ, who is your life, appears, then you also will appear with him in glory (3:1–4).

Already Paul has referred to their experience of "having been buried with Christ in baptism and raised with him through your faith in the power of God, who raised him from the dead" (2:12). Here he recalls once more their baptism and what it represented and signified in order to urge them to let their thoughts dwell on the heavenly realm where their Lord is enthroned.

This is a call to what today we would call serious meditation and contemplation. To help them live under the rule of Christ, as genuinely heavenly minded people, Paul urges them to reflect upon their baptism and its implications and to consider what it means in practice for them to be united to the enthroned and exalted Lord Jesus. Further, he urges them to consider what it means to be united to the Lord who will descend from heaven to earth to judge the living and the dead and who will place them at his right hand as his genuine sheep. If they reflect and consider in this manner, they will not set their standards and aims by what they see around them in the city of Colossae, but will seek to live as those who belong to heaven, putting to death evil desires and being clothed with compassion, kindness, humility, gentleness and patience. In this manner the peace of Christ will rule in their hearts, and his word will dwell richly in their minds, as they offer their whole lives to the exalted Lord Jesus, knowing that soon they will be with him.

Ephesians[11]

Here both the themes of the exaltation of Christ and of the Christian hope are prominent—as also is the triad of faith, hope and love. In fact, the concepts expressed in this Epistle are so profound that they deserve and demand prolonged consideration, which is possible when you take time to meditate upon them—as will be strongly recommended in chapter 9. Why not read it through slowly? When you do, you will find that heavenly-mindedness (which is the same as spiritual-mindedness) is the only appropriate attitude that committed Christians, united to an exalted Lord, ought to adopt.

The position of faithful (Gentile) believers is presented as being "fellow-citizens with God's people [Israel] and members of God's household, built on the foundation of the apostles and prophets, with Christ Jesus himself as the chief cornerstone" (2:19, 20). They are a necessary part of the spiritual temple that God is creating around Christ and by the Holy Spirit; and this temple is, as it were, growing up towards heaven to the One who is both its origin and source, its life and its inspiration. As Gentile believers they have become sharers together with Jewish believers in the promise originally made to Abraham and also heirs of the marvelous inheritance awaiting them in heaven. Furthermore, their inheritance is secure in heaven because Christ, their Representative, is there and in him they have been raised up to sit with him in the heavenly realms (2:6). Their life on earth is thus an upward movement to become in reality what they are already in Christ, their Head, whom God has placed in the position of supreme authority (1:20–23).

The only appropriate *primary* response to this knowledge is that which Paul cannot but offer as he begins the Letter: "Praise be to the God and Father of our Lord Jesus Christ, who has blessed us in the heavenly realms with every spiritual blessing in Christ . . ." (1:3). And this praise is not merely from the lips, it is from the heart and offered by the whole person, in whom is the Holy Spirit, who guarantees our inheritance until redemption is completed at the resurrection of the dead at the end of the age (1:14).

It is one thing to explain the great privileges of those who are in Christ, but it is another thing for those who have these privileges to appropriate, grasp and live in the light and strength of them. Thus Paul shares with the church members some of the major petitions he offers to God for them. "I keep asking that the God of our Lord Jesus Christ, the glorious Father, may give you the Spirit of wisdom and revelation, so that you may know him better" (1:17). Here "to know" is primarily, though not exclusively, knowing him as Father and praying " 'Abbā." And: "I pray also that the eyes of your heart may be enlightened in order that you may know the hope to which he has called you, the riches of his glorious inheritance in the saints and his incomparably great power for us who believe" (1:18–19). Here there is the recognition that we need heavenly illumination by the Holy Spirit in order rightly to think about heaven and what God has in store for us with Christ there. In a further prayer, Paul is overwhelmed by the magnitude of the love of God, which will be more fully appreciated and received in the heavenly realms: "I pray that you, being rooted and established in love, may have power, together with all the saints, to grasp how wide and long and high and deep is the love of Christ and to know this love surpassing knowledge— that you may be filled to the measure of all the fullness of God" (3:17b–19).

Apart from sharing the main petitions he offers on their behalf to heaven, Paul also, as is his method, urges them to live on earth as those who are truly citizens of the heavenly commonwealth. Christ is exalted and he has sent the Holy Spirit (and the gifts which he distributes) to the Church. Led and empowered by the Spirit, the people of God, which is the body of Christ, is to be built up in the faith and knowledge of the Gospel in order to become mature and heavenly minded (4:12ff.). They are not to live as their fellow Gentile pagans do, for their minds and hearts are darkened through sin and ignorance; but believers are to be imitators of God, living lives of love, and to act as children of light, manifesting goodness, righteousness and truth (5:1–10).

Finally, he calls upon them to remember that not only are they citizens of the heavenly commonwealth, but also they are soldiers in the army of the Lord. And this army is fighting Christ's war on earth; through the victory of the Cross, Resurrection and Exaltation, the decisive battle of the war between God and Satan has been won. However, the war will continue until the end of the age when Christ is revealed in power and glory from heaven. Therefore, those who are heavenly minded will be those who have put on the armor of God and taken hold of their sword. They will have the belt of truth, the breastplate of righteousness, the sandals of peace, the shield of faith and the helmet of salvation; and in their hands they will have the sword of the Spirit, which is the word of God. They will be alert, watching for the enemy both to defend themselves and to attack, knowing that the final victory is not far away.

We have hardly done justice to the dimension of heavenly-mindedness in Paul's Letters. However, what will have become clear through this short introduction are such themes as the importance of hope within the triad of faith, hope and love; the forward and upward thrust of Christian faith as it is united to hope and love; the duty of fixing one's thoughts upon the exalted, reigning Christ who will come; the great inheritance, confirmed by the inner witness of the Holy Spirit, which awaits the people of God in the kingdom of God; and the communion with and knowledge of, God as Father, which is real on earth and will be even more marvelous and personal in heaven.

If you are convinced by what is stated in the last paragraph, you could go straight to chapter 8 and be challenged to practice meditation upon heaven and develop thereby heavenly-mindedness. However, perhaps you would be wiser to follow the discipline of noting what other writers in the New Testament have to say about longing for the heavenly realm, since each one has his own particular emphasis—an emphasis that may have a special appeal to you or speak to you in a compelling manner.

5. A Better Country

We know that Jesus, as Messiah, fulfilled the Law and the Prophets. To Jewish Christians this fulfillment was of very special importance, for it was the very reason why they ceased to be Jews looking for the Messiah and became Jews who accepted Jesus as the true Messiah. The Letter to the Hebrews, or, as it may be called, "The Letter to the Jewish Christians," assumes a general knowledge of the Jewish Scriptures and Judaism in order to present in, with and through Jesus, as God's Son and Messiah, a better relationship (covenant) with God than either Abraham or Moses had known. Its author obviously lived with a personal faith which made him sure of what he hoped for and certain of what he could not see with his physical eyes (Heb. 11:1ff.). His whole thinking was dominated by his pilgrimage in the power of the Spirit of Christ towards Christ, who is seated at God's right hand in glory, and has there created a new "city and country" for the people of God of the new and old covenants.

Therefore, as you read slowly through this Letter to the Hebrews, you cannot fail to be moved by the claims made for Christ and the vitality of the faith and hope which are presented. Though parts may seem strange to you because you are not familiar with the Jewish and Old Testament background, you will soon feel within your soul that to be a Christian is to be a pilgrim journeying towards the city of God, where your Savior and Lord is. In this chapter we shall notice this longing for the heavenly city, where Christ is enthroned as our Priest and King, as we quickly work through the major themes of the Letter.[1] Since it was written for a Jewish readership—in contrast to Paul's writing for a predominantly Gentile readership—we may expect that old truth may hit us with new force.

Sonship

The Epistle opens with a long sentence (at least in the Greek text) in which the identity, nature and role of Christ are celebrated, and this is followed by an exposition of his Sonship in relation to the world of angels and mankind. He who, as Son, is greater than the greatest archangel became as man "a little lower than the angels . . . so that by the grace of God he might taste death for everyone" (2:9). And having written this, our anonymous author continues: "In bringing many sons to glory, it was fitting that God . . . should make the author of their salvation perfect through suffering. Both the one who makes men holy and those who are made holy are of the same family. So Jesus is not ashamed to call them brothers" (2:10–11).

The Incarnate Son is pleased to call believers his brothers and sisters because not only did he take as his own their human nature, but also he offered himself as a sacrifice for their sin so that they might be made holy (sanctified or set apart for God) and become adopted members of the family of God.

As the children of God and with Christ as "elder Brother," believers are on their way to glory, that glory which Jesus already enjoys in the heavenly realm. Though he does not use the word 'Abbā of God, our author is providing teaching wholly in harmony with that of Jesus and of Paul. Being set apart for God and consecrated to his service, as well as becoming the adopted children of God, Christians are to enjoy communion with God as they await perfect communion within the glory to come.

In the transition from the theme of Sonship (chapters 1 and 2) to that of the Sabbath-rest of the people of God (chapters 3 and 4), we read these words: "Therefore, holy brothers, who share in the heavenly calling, fix your thoughts on Jesus, the apostle and high priest whom we confess" (3:1).

Jesus is God's representative before mankind and mankind's representative before God, since he is both apostle (the one sent) and High Priest. As those who are called by God into both his service here on earth and into the hope of sharing his glory, we have a heavenly calling. Paul had urged his converts to set their hearts on the heavenly realm where Christ is enthroned; much the same advice is given here. *We are to make time to fix our thoughts upon the Lord Jesus and to contemplate what it means for us to have a Savior and Lord in such a position.*

Rest

In his presentation of the Sabbath-rest of God, our author seems to be speaking of things which are far away from our modern experience. This has not always been so. The well-known seventeenth-century writer Richard Baxter wrote a long and important book entitled *The Saints' Everlasting Rest*.[2] In his day, people worked hard and had little rest: most jobs involved hard physical labor. Thus the presentation of heaven as the place of rest was appealing at the straightforward level to tired and often diseased people. However, Baxter was well aware that the Sabbath-rest of God is much more than the cessation from hard physical labor and from deprivation, disease and disorder.

The rest of God into which we enter and will fully know in the life of the age to come has a positive side. God created the world in six days, and then on the seventh day he rested and thereby instituted the Sabbath as the day of rest. God's rest involved his positive contemplation of what he had made and his recognition that it was all good. "There remains, then, a Sabbath-rest for the people of God; for anyone who enters God's rest also rests from his own work, just as God did from his" (4:9–10). When we have completed our assigned task for God in this world, then we enter into God's rest, that is, we are taken up into the life and glory of God to participate in his contemplation of his creation old and new and his joy that it is good. Christ himself has entered into this rest and we are to join him. It is significant that Christ lay at rest on the Sabbath between Good Friday and Easter Day; as he lay at rest, he looked upon the travail of his soul, which resulted in

the provision of salvation for the world, and was satisfied, as he also eagerly awaited his exaltation into God's
heavenly rest. *Being "in Christ," we are already experiencing aspects of "heavenly rest": the taste should
make us long for the fullness.*

Melchizedek

The next theme is that of Christ, our exalted high
priest, who is our perfect Representative in heaven, and
who is of the order of Melchizedek (for whom see
Genesis 14 and Psalm 110:4).[3] In the course of this
discussion (which requires some knowledge of the Old
Testament to appreciate fully), we read:

> Because God wanted to make the unchanging nature of his
> purpose very clear to the heirs of what was promised, he
> confirmed it with an oath. God did this so that, by two
> unchangeable things in which it is impossible for God to lie,
> we who have fled to take hold of the hope offered to us may
> be greatly encouraged. We have this hope as an anchor for
> the soul, firm and secure. It enters the inner sanctuary
> behind the curtain, where Jesus, who went before us, has
> entered on our behalf (Heb. 6:17–20).

Being members of God's family, we are heirs, joint heirs
with Christ, of the kingdom and glory and rest of God. In
faith, we trust in God's promises of grace and salvation,
promises which are, as it were, underlined by his own
oath (Ps. 110:4). Therefore, we have "two unchangeable
things" on which to rely. *We flee from this present
world, which is like a sinking ship, and we cling to the
hope of a better and heavenly world promised in the*

Gospel. This hope is as an anchor which is firmly fastened to an immovable rock; it is secured to Jesus himself, who is already in heaven (here described with reference to the holy of holies of the Temple, which was protected by a curtain or veil).

New Covenant

From the discussion of the High Priesthood of Christ, the Letter proceeds to explain that a new covenant between God and mankind has been established through the sacrificial blood of Jesus: this is the covenant described by the prophet Jeremiah (Jer. 31:31–34) in which the human membership will know God, that is, have communion and fellowship with God. Because he believes that his readers, as Christians, are within this new covenant, he exhorts them (us) in this manner: "Therefore, brothers, since we have confidence to enter the Most Holy Place by the blood of Jesus, by a new and living way opened for us through the curtain, that is, his body, and since we have a great high priest over the house of God, let us draw near to God with a sincere heart in full assurance of faith, having our hearts sprinkled to cleanse us from a guilty conscience and having our bodies washed with pure water" (Heb. 10:19–22).

In the old covenant, only the high priest could enter the most holy place and then only once a year; Jesus has entered into heaven and he calls us into communion with heaven, having provided in his sacrificial blood the basis for our entry, our cleansing and our fellowship with God. We, as those baptized (our bodies washed) into this new covenant, have received an outward and visible sign of an inward and spiritual change: the barrier that kept us from heaven and from fellowship with the living God has been taken away through the atonement of Christ.

Our author's exhortation does not stop with this call to draw near to God, which is a daily joy and duty: he continues by speaking of hope:

> Let us hold unswervingly to the hope we profess, for he who promised is faithful. And let us consider how we may spur one another on towards love and good deeds. Let us not give up meeting together, as some are in the habit of doing, but let us encourage one another—and all the more as you see the Day approaching (10:23–25).

We are to draw near to God "in full assurance of faith" and at the same time to "hold unswervingly to the hope we profess," not forgetting the practical "love and good deeds." Such are the pressures of pagan or secularist society that there is always the temptation to swerve from the contemplation of the hope of the kingdom of heaven to the hope merely of better earthly existence.

Yet, since it is the living God, eternal and infinite, who has revealed himself to us in his Incarnate Son, and through him made many, wonderful promises, we surely ought and must hold unswervingly to the hope contained in the Gospel. Further, this hope is a hope of a kingdom of pure love, and thus, since our eyes are fixed on this love of God, we ought to be employed on earth (as we wait) in the loving of our neighbor in such practical ways as the situation warrants and requires. And since our hope is that of belonging to a new family in a new creation in order to praise and worship the

Lord, then the anticipation and celebration of that in the fellowship and worship of the local church ought to be encouraged and enjoyed.

Here is a paradox of grace. The more intensely the hope of being with Christ in heaven burns in our hearts, the more vigorously do we love our neighbor and experience the foretaste of heaven in celebratory worship.

Faith

We have now arrived at chapter 11, which is often described as the chapter of faith. And so it is; but it is also about faith and hope, for it is faith which cannot be prized apart from hope. This is how it begins: "Now faith is being sure of what we hope for and certain of what we do not see. This is what the ancients were commended for" (11:1–2). The Lord gave promise of what he would do in the future to the patriarchs; these people then acted as if what was promised for the future was actually present, because they were surely convinced that God would fulfill what he had promised. What was in historical terms future as well as invisible, they saw as present to their eyes of faith and acted accordingly. Thus the patriarchs or ancients were commended by God for their faith and hope together.

After providing the examples of Abel, Enoch and Noah, the following is said of Abraham by way of illustrating his faith and hope:

By faith Abraham, when called to go to a place he would later receive as his inheritance, obeyed and went, even though he did not know where he was going. By faith he made his home in the promised land like a stranger in a foreign country; he lived in tents, as did Isaac and Jacob, who were heirs with him of the same promise. For he was looking forward to the city with foundations, whose architect and builder is God (11:8–10).

To appreciate what is said of Abraham, the modern reader must look at Genesis 11ff. and especially at such promises as those in 12:1–4 and 15:1–6—which will only be truly and finally fulfilled in the new people of God of the new covenant in the new creation of the new age to come.

In his faith and hope Abraham was looking for a special kind of city, a heavenly Jerusalem, in a heavenly country. In ancient times the great city was seen as a place of safety, security and peace where the people lived under the strict but paternal rule of the king; for us the city has become the symbol of decadence, decay and deprivation. *We have to appreciate that the city was a symbol of strength, harmony and security for ancient people and thus a fitting analogy for God's new order in the kingdom of heaven; for such a city Abraham and the patriarchs hoped. And so ought we!*

The theme of the city returns a little later at the end of the paragraph which we shall now quote:

All these people were still living by faith when they died. They did not receive the things promised; they only saw them and welcomed them from a distance. And they admitted that they were aliens and strangers on earth. People who say such things show that they are looking for a country of their own. If they had been thinking of the country they had left, they would have had opportunity to return. Instead they were longing for a better country—a heavenly one. There-

fore God is not ashamed to be called their God, for he has
prepared a city for them (11:13–16).

It is certainly true that the people who descended from
Abraham received the promised land of Canaan and the
great city of Jerusalem. But these were merely important material symbols and signposts, pointing to the far
greater reality of the heavenly country towards the
heavenly city (the realities portrayed in the visions
of Revelation 21 and 22). The people of faith were
the heirs of God's promise, the promise of a new
heavenly cosmos in which would be perfect joy, peace
and righteousness in the immediate presence of the
God of glory.

And since their eyes were set upon this heavenly
reality, in relation to human civilization they were as
aliens and strangers. Not that they did not care about
human life on earth (a careful study of the law of
Moses reveals how carefully human life was to be regu-
lated in purity and wholeness); but that their greater
care was the hope of the better city and country. At the
end of his celebration of faith and faithfulness in chapter 11, our author concludes: "These were all commended
for their faith, yet none of them received what had been
promised. God had planned something better for us so
that only together with us would they be made perfect"
(11:39–40). Now these people of faith are in heaven,
looking upon God in the face of Jesus Christ and receiving all the benefits of the new covenant. And, like us,
they will be members of the new age and kingdom of
God after the Parousia of Christ.

Inheritance

The next theme, that of God disciplining his adopted sons (children) in order that they will come to their inheritance and not fall away, is introduced with a "therefore" (12:1) and proceeds, against the background of the great celebration of faith and hope in chapter 11, in this way:

> Since we are surrounded by such a great cloud of witnesses, let us throw off everything that hinders and the sin that so easily entangles, and let us run with perseverance the race marked out for us. Let us fix our eyes on Jesus, the author and perfector of our faith, who for the joy set before him endured the cross, scorning its shame, and sat down at the right hand of the throne of God (12:1–2).

The Christian life is portrayed here as like running a race. The athlete when in training is disciplined in what he eats and does because he wants his whole self, body and mind, to be fit and intent on winning the race and gaining the prize. Jesus himself had before him the joy of heaven as he gladly and patiently accomplished the will of the Father on earth. Therefore the Christian, contemplating his enthroned Lord and example, is to live in such a way as to prepare himself for heavenly life. Thus everything that is sinful and much that is, in itself, acceptable or good have to be avoided in order to maintain and deepen fellowship with God and obedience to his will.

Later in the chapter, our author, recalling how the Israelites came first to Mount Sinai and then to Mount Zion, reminds his readers how by their conversion and baptism they have come to the heavenly realm, to the new Mount Zion. He explains:

> But you have come to Mount Zion, to the heavenly Jerusa-
> lem, the city of the living God. You have come to thousands
> upon thousands of angels in joyful assembly, to the church
> of the first-born, whose names are written in heaven. You
> have come to God, the judge of all men, to the spirits of
> righteous men made perfect, to Jesus the mediator of a new
> covenant, and to the sprinkled blood that speaks a better
> word than the blood of Abel (12:22–24).

The earthly Zion was the meeting point for the tribes
of Israel and for their worship of the Lord in the temple
there; thus Zion was the center of the city of Jerusalem
(Ps. 78:68ff.; 122:3ff.). The Temple and the City were
seen here as material copies of the heavenly archetypes—
the heavenly city which is presented in Revelation 21 as
waiting to descend to earth. *Through faith and union
with the exalted Jesus, Christians already have access
to this heavenly city or realm and already in faith
enjoy the privileges of citizenship.* In this heavenly
realm there are myriads of angels (cf. Dt. 33:2; Dn.
7:10) engaged in the worship and service of the Lord;
here also (as viewed "in Christ," as Paul taught) is the
totality of those who are the Church of God, since,
being raised and exalted in Christ, they exist there in
Christ's Representation of them, before individually they
actually arrive. It is this totality whose names are written in heaven, in the Lamb's book of life (Lk. 10:20;
Rev. 21:27). Among those who have already arrived
are the faithful of the old covenant, "the righteous men
made perfect."

But what makes the heavenly realm truly to be the
heavenly realm is that here believers encounter God,
the Judge, in and through Jesus, the Mediator. As the
eternal Son he brings God to them, and as Man he

takes them to God; and he does this because by his atonement he has dealt fully and decisively with the problem of their sin.

If you have only absorbed a portion of the heavenly-mindedness presented in this Letter, you will surely confess: "Here we do not have an enduring city, but we are looking for the city that is to come" (13:14). You are a pilgrim moving carefully towards this city, seeking as you go to keep your eyes fixed upon it and to live as a faithful disciple. You desire to take other people along with you in this pilgrimage in order that they will escape from the judgment that God has passed on this present world and evil age, and enjoy fellowship, love and peace with you and all saints with Christ in heaven.

A characteristic of genuine pilgrims is that their journey is dominated by thoughts of their goal and by intense desires to reach it. May Christians call themselves pilgrims if they do not actually daily long for the heavenly realm?

6. A Living and Purifying Hope

We have seen how both in the Letters of Paul and in the Letter to the Hebrews, the possession of genuine hope within the believer's heart has the effect of changing his direction, character and attitude. This is also well recognized by Peter and John in their Letters. To Peter, hope was alive and vigorous, promoting the right direction and attitude in the Christian life and community; to John, hope was purifying, causing the putting aside of that which hinders and taking on board that which assists pilgrimage.

As we examine various texts in the Letters of Peter and John, we shall inevitably find ourselves repeating what has already been said and noticed. If such repetition needs justifying, it may be done on the basis that frequently the New Testament itself exhorts us to be people of faith, hope and love as we journey towards heaven.

Peter opens his First Letter by calling the Christians, to whom he writes, "God's elect, strangers in the world" who are scattered in different places.[1] Obviously, he does not consider that his readers are in their true homeland but are, rather, temporarily dispersed in this world as they wait to enter their true home, the heavenly Jerusalem. And the reason why they belong to another world than this present sinful world is because of the grace of God in choosing them, making atonement for their sins, and making them holy by the indwelling Spirit.

After the opening address, Peter shares a prayer of praise and thanksgiving with his readers:

> Praise be to the God and Father of our Lord Jesus Christ! In his great mercy he has given us new birth into a living hope through the resurrection of Jesus Christ from the dead, and into an inheritance that can never perish, spoil or fade—kept in heaven for you, who through faith are shielded by God's power until the coming of the salvation that is ready to be revealed in the last time (1 Pet.1:3–5).

The new birth is an internal change caused by the Holy Spirit as the sinner responds to the message of the resurrection of Jesus through the Gospel. "You have been born again, not of perishable seed, but of imperishable, through the living and enduring word of God" (1:23). Christians are those who have experienced the new birth to become members of a new creation which is the kingdom of God; thus they have been born into both "a living hope" and "an inheritance that can never perish, spoil or fade."

The hope into which Christians are born is alive, vigorous and healthy. Since it rests upon the living God who cannot fail, it is truly a hope by which one may truly and fully live. It is to be contrasted to hope of better things, place or situation within this world; because of a variety of uncertainties, any hope geared to this world cannot be healthy, for it must always be nagged by doubts of failure. The inheritance into which Christians are born cannot be affected by death, evil or time. It is imperishable, unspoilt and unfading because it already exists in heaven. The use of this image of inheritance goes back to the old covenant, where God gave the Israelites the land of Canaan as their earthly inheritance. Yet this portion of Near Eastern land pointed to a greater inheritance for the people of God (Ps. 16:5, 6; 73:26). Thus it is not surprising that in the New Testament the image is used to point to that which God has in store for his people when they enter heaven (cf. Mk. 10:17; 1 Cor. 6:9; 15:50; Col. 3:24; Tit. 3:7; Heb. 1:14).

Indwelt by the Spirit, guided by hope of what shall surely be and looking forward to the inheritance of the people of God, Christians are on the highway to salvation, that is, to participation in the consummation of God's purposes in the life of the age to come. As they trust in the Lord, his power guards and shields them so that they are protected not from facing difficulties and trials but from falling prey to temptation and demonic assault.

This prayer makes clear that the movement of the Christian life is to be through this world towards God's promised inheritance; this means that the direction of life is both upward and onward, since heaven, which is now "above," is also future in and through the Parousia of Christ. The temporary nature of life in this world and age comes out in the rest of the prayer:

In this [hope of salvation] you greatly rejoice, though now for a little while you may have had to suffer grief in all kinds of trials. These have come so that your faith—of greater worth than gold, which perishes even though refined by fire—may be proved genuine and may result in praise, glory and honor when Jesus Christ is revealed. Though you have not seen him, you love him; and even though you do not see him now, you believe in him and are filled with an inexpressible and glorious joy, for you are receiving the goal of your faith, the salvation of your souls (1:6–9).

Christians rejoice and continue to rejoice through hardships and difficulties because of the sure and living hope that God has given them in Christ and the promises of the Gospel. The joy that is known now, even in persecution, is the joy of life in the new creation of God's kingdom; it is the joy of the "last days" anticipated in the present.

Faith to be also faithfulness has to go to school to learn, and there is nothing like trials and persecution to provide the setting in which spiritual learning can take place. Christians are to have their eyes fixed upon the exalted Lord Jesus as they live faithfully for him in this world, awaiting his return. For when he comes they will be clothed in their new resurrection bodies for life with Christ, whom they love, in the age to come.

Again we see in this portion of Scriptures how faith (that is faithful), hope (that is sure and lively) and love (of Christ and his people) belong together in this age, flowing into and out of each other within the Christian pilgrimage towards the homeland of the age to come. And this is true of the rest of the Letter, portions of which we shall proceed to examine.

In the second chapter Peter describes the Christian

communities in a series of rich images as "a chosen people, a royal priesthood, a holy nation, a people belonging to God" who are to praise him (2:9). Then he writes: "I urge you as aliens and strangers in the world, to abstain from sinful desires which war against your soul" (2:11). Earlier we noted how Christians are separated or exiled from their homeland and are on a journey towards it. Here the other side of this truth is emphasized. Christians are not at home in this world, for its culture, ethos and standards are affected by Satan, sin and evil; they feel they are in a foreign land because their values and aspirations are so different from those of the people among whom they live. But, as Peter states, it is not enough to feel that you are different; you are actually to be different not only externally but also internally —"be holy because I am holy" (1:16). Christians reveal that they are foreigners in this world by the quality of their lives as well as by the hope that they possess (3:15).

In chapter 4 Peter explains that it is a great privilege to suffer as a Christian and thus bear the shame of Christ. In fact, he wrote very personally as "a witness of Christ's suffering and one who also will share in the glory to be revealed," and then, speaking to the pastors of the churches he is addressing, he writes: "And when the Chief Shepherd appears, you will receive the crown of glory that will never faded away" (5:1, 4). He looks forward to the Parousia and to the inheritance of everlasting life in the kingdom of God both for the pastors and for himself, who, with them, is a shepherd under the Chief Shepherd. And the Letter comes to a fitting ending with the prayer: "And the God of all grace, who called you to his eternal glory in Christ, after you have suffered a little while, will himself restore you and make you strong, firm and steadfast. To him be the power for ever and ever, Amen" (5:10).

In the Second Letter of Peter there is much emphasis upon the future coming of the Lord Jesus to bring to an end this world and age.[2] Concerning what will be after the judgment of the nations, we read: "But in keeping with his promise we are looking forward to a new heaven and a new earth, the home of righteousness" (3:13). Here the prophecy of Isaiah (65:17ff.) is recalled and the hope expressed of the new cosmos, which will be heaven and homeland for the new people of God. Jesus himself had made reference to this cosmic renewal (Mt. 19:28); just as there is a personal regeneration, a birth into life, hope and an inheritance, so there is to be a cosmic regeneration, as the last chapters of the Book of Revelation so beautifully portray, and, as Paul explained, the present creation was itself longing for (Rom. 8:18ff.). Into such a living hope we as Christians have entered.

Purifying Hope

As Peter describes a living hope, so John describes a purifying hope.[3] Here is how he expresses it:

> How great is the love that the Father has lavished on us, that we should be called children of God! And that is what we are! The reason the world does not know us is that it did not know him. Dear friends, now we are the children of God, and what we will be has not yet been made known. But we know that when he appears, we shall be like him, for we shall see

him as he is. Everyone who has this hope in him purifies himself, just as he is pure (3:1–3).

There is a great emphasis in 1 John on God's love for us and within us: "This is love; not that we loved God, but that he loved us and sent his Son as an atoning sacrifice for our sins" (4:10). Thus we love him and our fellow human beings because he first loved us.

It is because God's love is so rich towards us that he calls us, as believers in his Son, his children. Having been called by the Gospel, we have been adopted into his heavenly family as his adopted children. We have been born of God through the coming of the Holy Spirit into our lives (3:9; 4:7), and thus we have eternal life (2:25) and fellowship with the Father and the Son (1:3). We are, first and foremost, before all other considerations, the children of God who are to reflect the "family likeness" by walking in the light, by loving God and the members of the Christian fellowship, and by refusing to conform to the standards and values of pagan society. We belong to heaven because that is where our Father and our Lord Jesus Christ are.

Thus, as members of a family which belongs to the heavenly realm, not to this world, we long to enjoy to the full the family life of which now we only have a foretaste. We look for the Parousia of Christ, knowing that this will be the occasion for the arrival of the enjoyment of eternal life within our new resurrection bodies as part of the new creation. We are therefore a people with a living and dynamic hope; and, as such, we live today as those who really do have such a hope. Christ is our example, and as he is pure in heart, so it is our aim, as we do his will and patiently wait for his Parousia, to be pure in heart so that we shall truly see God.

Though Peter and John have different styles and use different images, what they teach is, in essence, the same concerning the Christian hope. For each writer the possibility of being a committed Christian and not having a lively and purifying hope would have been a nonstarter. For them the triad of faith, hope and love belonged together because they saw living in this world as only a preparation for living in the kingdom of God of the age to come. Living with and for Christ now definitely included waiting for his Parousia and longing for the heavenly realm.

We have now come to the end of the survey of biblical teaching. Since it is so easy to treat biblical knowledge as any other kind of knowledge, it would perhaps be a wise step at this stage to spend a little time in prayer, asking the Lord to help you to assimilate this knowledge in such a way that it enters your heart as well as your mind. One ancient prayer which may be helpful is:

> Almighty God, we thank you for the gift of your holy word. May it be a lantern to our feet, and a light to our paths, and a strength to our lives. Take us and use us to love and serve all men in the power of the Holy Spirit, and in the name of your Son, Jesus Christ, our Lord. Amen.

Another, traditionally said on Ascension Day, is:

> Almighty God, as we believe your only-begotten Son, our Lord Jesus Christ, to have ascended into heaven, so may we

also in heart and mind thither ascend and with him continually dwell; who is alive and reigns with you and the Holy Spirit, one God, now and for ever. Amen.

Finally, as you are aware of the particular pressures of our consumer oriented and secularized society, you may want to pray:

O Lord God, the protector of all who trust in you, without whom nothing is strong, nothing is holy: increase and multiply upon us your mercy, that you being our ruler and guide, we may so pass through things temporal that we finally lose not the things eternal. Grant this, heavenly Father, for the sake of Jesus Christ, our Lord.

Instructed by the word of the Lord, and looking to him for his illumination and help, you are now ready to proceed to the tough discipline of meditation upon "the things eternal."

PART II

7. Obstacles
and Hindrances

In order to proceed, certain assumptions must be made. I shall assume that the careful reader of the New Testament, and of this book, accepts that hope is integral to authentic (in contrast to nominal) Christianity. He or she recognizes that believers were urged by the apostolic writers to wait patiently for the Parousia and the revelation of the glory of the Lord as they willingly proceeded with the task of serving Christ faithfully day by day. Thus hope of receiving full salvation and a glorious inheritance in the kingdom of heaven in the communion of saints and with Christ is basic and fundamental to the profession of the Faith in this world. So it is that Christians are aptly described as exiles from their homeland and aliens, strangers and pilgrims on this earth, since they belong to a heavenly and better country.

Heavenly-mindedness is, therefore, a necessary part of the Christian outlook and approach to life and death. This world and the things within it must be set against the heavenly world where Christ is enthroned, for only in this comparison can a proper evaluation of the things of this world be made. Unless Christians are living in the light of Christ, who is above, guided by his Spirit, which comes from above bringing his mind to us, then they must be living in the light of this world, guided by one or other of its philosophies or ideologies. No person can serve two masters, and it is not possible to be truly heavenly minded and truly worldly minded simultaneously. Either life in this world is viewed in the light from heaven, or heaven is viewed in the light from this world.

If this be so, then those of us who accept the authority of the sacred Scriptures as the rule of faith and life must ask ourselves how are we to recover this primitive Christian sense of living in hope, waiting to enter into the glory of God, and longing to do so. There are positive steps we can take, and to these we turn in chapter 9. Also, there are obstacles over which we must jump or which we must avoid; and there are hindrances that must be removed or put away. We shall look first at five obstacles and then seven hindrances. You may be aware of others not mentioned here.

Five Obstacles

1. *Perhaps strange to relate, much biblical scholarship stands in our way.* If you read the great number of books produced by scholars whose expertise is the study

of the New Testament, you will find in them valuable information and insights on a vast range of minor matters, from the meaning of obscure phrases to the dating of a particular book. Much of what you read will be one scholar putting forward his latest view, and showing how the views of others, who have worked in this particular field of study, are faulty. This has its place, but what is missing in the provision by scholars is material which truly raises the spiritual and moral aspirations of the Church of God, to whose service many scholars claim to devote themselves.

If you spend too much time studying the usual products of contemporary scholarship, you are hardly likely to be fired with a living and purifying hope of the Lord's Parousia. You are more likely to lose the vision in the clouds of questions, problems and uncertainties raised by the books and learned articles you read. Regrettably, you may well have to conclude that most New Testament scholars appear to serve the industry and perpetuation of New Testament scholarship and not the edification of the people of God.[1]

2. *If you do begin to think seriously of the Parousia of Jesus, you will have to face the repeated claim within books about the New Testament that both Jesus himself and his apostles expected that it would occur within a few years of his Ascension.* And often accompanying this claim will be the further suggestions that (a) Jesus and the apostles were wrong in their expectation of the Parousia as the way of bringing this age to an end, and (b) the whole primitive Christian views of heaven and hope of the Parousia have to be demythologized. However, what is left after this process of demythologization has been done (and there is not

any agreed way of doing it) is not a faith that would inspire people to suffer as martyrs or face continued hardship and tribulation for what they believe and hope for.

In response to these obstacles, it is possible to argue that belief in the Parousia and heavenly realm is not affected even if it could be proved that Jesus and the apostles believed that the Parousia would occur earlier rather than later. Further, it is possible to argue that, while the belief in the second coming of Christ from heaven is certainly couched in strange (i.e., apocalyptic) language, nevertheless it remains a real hope which must be expressed in language heavily dependent upon image and metaphor.[2]

3. *You will find that there is such a tremendous emphasis within the contemporary churches on improving the lot of people in this world that you feel out of place, perhaps even odd, if you ask questions about the heavenly realm.* Not only in the publications from such bodies as the World Council of Churches but also from some evangelical groups there has come in recent decades a great commitment to social justice with "a bias towards the poor." The danger in this is that of making salvation a this-worldly experience and of removing from the Church both the good news of heaven above and the call of the Gospel to live in hope of an eternal inheritance. And this social emphasis is usually found in churches where it is rare to hear a sermon on heaven and rarer still a sermon on hell.

Of course, it is part of the Christian love of the neighbor in God's world to be concerned about the social condition of people; but this emphasis is subsidiary to that of the call to become children of God and heirs of heaven. We are to preach the Gospel within the context of caring for the whole person in his or her environment; we are to offer membership in the kingdom of heaven. It is not social service and concern *or* proclamation of the promise of heaven; it is both together. It is true that if the churches turn a blind eye to the suffering and needs of people, they must not be surprised if these people are deaf to their message; thus mission includes both evangelism and social service. Heaven is the goal of both! A good thing must not be an obstacle to the best thing.[3]

4. *Then, whatever be your educational background, you must be prepared to think for yourself in matters pertaining to the health of your soul.* Certainly, not a little of the contemporary Christian paperback output presumes that people cannot really think for themselves and spoon-feeds them with instructions on how to do this and that.

The danger is that the profoundly simple Gospel becomes a non-Gospel, a simplistic Gospel. In contrast to this modern tendency, it is quite amazing that many ordinary Christians without intellectual training are enabled, when given the right encouragement and context, in the power of the Spirit to think deeply about God and spiritual matters. This gift ought to be encouraged rather than ignored; people must not be treated as if they were only capable of responding to being told how to do this or that.

You must be prepared to think seriously not only about God, his character and his will but also about the world as the arena in which you are to do the will of God. You are called to love God with all your heart, mind and strength, and this means that you must know who it is that you are loving and what is his will for you, a sinner who is longing to be holy and to attain blessedness as you see the Lord in heaven.

5. *Finally, you ought to reflect upon, and be ready to reject, the pressure to be active, to be up and off and doing something.*[4] Though we have better transport to get us from here to there more quickly and with less tiredness, and though we possess a host of labor-saving devices, we seem to have less time for people and certainly less time for God. So many Christians are so busy attending this or that meeting and supporting this or that Christian cause that they have no time left for prayer and meditation. They may have time for a quick quiet time or for saying a few prayers; but they have no time for waiting upon the Lord and for being still, in order to know that he is truly God. One problem with bible-reading aids and such like is that they can encourage the speedy entrance into the quiet place and the hasty exit from that place of encounter with heaven. For once you have done what is suggested, you have done your duty. Activism is an obstacle to purity of heart and to desire for the heavenly realm.

Seven Hindrances

The athlete whose leg is heavily bandaged is unable to run as fast as he would wish; the housewife whose wrist is broken cannot do her work in the kitchen as quickly or as well as she would wish. The Christian who is a pilgrim on the highway to Zion can be slowed down—even turned aside or around—by hindrances which affect the health of his or her soul. Here, for

your consideration, are examples of seven such hindrances which will impede the journey of the one in
whose life they are found. Perhaps some apply to you.

*1. Are you living in a particular sin of which you are
conscious and have not repented?*   Regrettably, preparation for heaven must include talk of sin, for heaven is
the sphere from where sin has been banished. If you
are experiencing a continuing sense of guilt concerning
something your conscience clearly tells you is sin, then
you are not making progress in the heavenly life. Such
a sin could be a sin of omission—neglecting a known
duty in the home, at work or in church; or it could be a
sin of commission—continuing to do something that
you know to be wrong. Consciousness of known and
unrepented sin is a great impediment in the heart of the
Christian, since it affects his or her whole being and not
least his or her relationship with the heavenly Father.
"If we confess our sins, he is faithful and just and will
forgive us our sins and purify us from all unrighteous-
ness" (Jn. 1:9).

*2. Is making money, amassing possessions or a related
pursuit more important to you than rejoicing in hope
of the glory of God?*   Does God take second place to
Mammon? Consider the parable of the rich fool (Lk.
12:13ff.) and his claim: "I'll say to myself, 'You have
plenty of good things laid up for many years. Take life
easy; eat, drink and be marry.' " And the reply of God:
"You fool! This very night your life will be demanded
from you . . ." Then also remember the practical wisdom of James: "Don't you know that friendship with
the world is hatred towards God? Anyone who chooses
to be a friend of the world becomes an enemy of God"
(Jas. 4:4). In God's providence, money and possessions

may come your way but they do so in order that you may be a steward of them, using them to his glory, not to yours. Do not allow them to prevent you walking upward towards your Lord.

3. *Do you spend a lot of time in the company of those who make no time for the worship of God and the seeking of his kingdom?* Do you aim to keep up with the Joneses, not only in the furnishing of your house but also in the attendance at or giving of parties? Too many Christians place themselves in positions of compromise and difficulty because they feel that they must fit into a social role—which they assume is required of them—if they are to be regarded as nice and decent people. And in assuming such a role they are forced into conversations and situations which severely strain or negate their Christian profession. We are to be in the world but not of the world: it is possible to be a good neighbor and faithful citizen without being forced into positions of compromise. We have to learn graciously to say "No" at an early stage to invitations which we know will lead us into such situations. "Self-control" is one of the fruits of the Spirit (Gal. 5:23), and it is needed if you are to remain a genuine pilgrim.

4. *Do you regularly engage in arguments about minor religious questions or grumble about this or that moral problem?* It is so easy to allow the profession of Christianity to become the advocacy of your (right) opinions. "Avoid foolish controversies . . . because these are unprofitable and useless" (Tit. 3:9; cf. 1 Tim. 6:3–5). Those who want to walk uprightly on the highway of holiness will concern themselves with such doctrines and teaching as assist them in their struggle upward to Zion. Keep clear of arguments which you know have no practical bearing on the Christian life.

5. Have you a proud and haughty spirit? It was pride, we recall, that led to the expulsion of the angels from heaven, and it is pride that will keep your heart from heaven. "Clothe yourselves with humility, towards one another, because 'God opposes the proud but gives grace to the humble.' Humble yourselves, therefore, under God's mighty hand, that he may lift you up in due time" (1 Pet. 5:5–6). Are you the kind of person who is elated when people speak well of you and highly dejected when you hear a word of criticism made against you? Are you quickly angry if your word or will is crossed and challenged? Are you much more ready to justify yourself than to engage in self-examination and confession? To enter the kingdom of heaven, you must become as a little child.

6. Have you a slothful, indolent spirit in spiritual matters? It is possible to know much and be outwardly charming and yet be slothful in spirit. Heaven, as it were, is above, and to travel there is a difficult and steep ascent, which takes discipline, determination and resolution. Too many people who practice religion sit at the bottom of the hill and occasionally look up to say what a pleasant sight is the heavenly hill! They admire the view but make little or no effort to climb up there. As Jesus said, it is the forceful, determined people who are the ones who lay hold of the kingdom of heaven (Mt. 11:12). To climb this mountainous road to Zion, you must become single-minded and wholly committed to your goal.

7. Are you contented with preparation for the heavenly life or, maybe, with the foretaste of it available here on earth? Be clear that to discuss heaven, to study the doctrine of heaven or to preach on heaven will not, in and of itself, get you near or into heaven. You discuss, study and preach because God, in grace, has first given you faith to believe him, love to adore him, and hope to desire him. Further, be aware that there is a very subtle temptation facing middle-class or affluent Christians who are members of lively or charismatic congregations to be satisfied with their experience (which is a combination of the benefits of the affluent society and the presence and power of the Spirit) here and now and thus to have little or no longing or desire for the heavenly realm. Where there is a happy, caring fellowship with evidence of the presence and power and gifts of the Spirit of Christ, and where this exists alongside a fine home with everything that the consumer society and modern medical services offer, then it can seem that this combined experience is great and ought to last for ever and ever. Be warned: only the kingdom of heaven lasts forever and should be sought.

Alongside the facing of obstacles and removing of hindrances, there must be the encouragement of a new, inner spiritual force that will generate a living and purifying hope. One tried and tested way of acquiring this is to engage in the practice of meditation or contemplation of the exalted Lord Jesus in heaven.

8. Meditation: What Is It?

The Biblical Basis

"Blessed is the man who does not walk in the counsel of the wicked or stand in the way of sinners, or sit in the seat of mockers. But his delight is in the law of the LORD, and on his law he meditates day and night" (Ps. 1:1–2). This is how the book of Psalms begins; a contrast is made between what the godly person avoids and what is the center of his life. His whole existence is centered upon, and flows from, his meditation upon the written word of God recorded in the five books of Moses. He is not a recluse but a man of action, whose action originates in meditation upon God's revealed will recorded in Scripture.

There is an echo in these verses of one of the commands given by God to Joshua when he became the leader of the people of Israel. God said to him: "Do not let this Book of the Law depart from your mouth; meditate on it day and night, so that you may be careful to do everything written in it" (Jos. 1:8). Joshua was not being told to spend all day and night in reflection upon God's self-revelation and the commands he had given to Moses: he was being told that at any time of day or night it was appropriate to think deeply and seriously about what God had said and what his will required in the life of the people. He was not to lead the people into any action until he had carefully thought about God and his will for them. As we shall see, what applied to Joshua and was repeated by the psalmist also applies to each one of us: each of us has a duty to meditate in the presence of the Lord upon what the Lord has revealed. Only by doing this shall it be said of any of us: "He is like a tree planted by streams of water, which yields its fruit in season and whose leaf does not wither" (Ps. 1:3).

Meditation is not prayer, though it is closely related to prayer and may either lead to it or begin from it. It is easy to talk about meditation but less easy actually to engage in meditation. Yet it is a spiritual discipline which has always been practiced by saintly people, whether they belonged to the old or new covenant and whether they were trained intellectually or not. "Oh, how I love your law! I meditate on it all day long," exclaimed the psalmist, who proceeded humbly to claim, "I have more insight than all my teachers for I meditate on your statutes" (Ps. 119:97, 99). Meditation not only brings insight into the nature and implications of God's revealed will, but also it fires the soul with zeal to do the will of the Lord joyfully and sincerely.

In English translations of the Greek New Testament, the words "meditate" and "meditation" are rarely, if ever, used. However, this does not mean that meditation, as practiced by Joshua and the psalmists, ceased with the arrival of the Messiah. It is not the case that meditation was replaced by proclamation and activism. Meditation was linked to proclamation, evangelism and mission as the source of the convictions and assurance of those who proclaimed, evangelized and engaged in mission. When apostles, evangelists and prophets spent time in fasting and prayer, we are to understand that they also engaged in meditation. Further, when we read the apostolic writings, we are constantly being exhorted to meditate through such words as "consider" (Phil. 2:3), "take such a view" (3:15), "take note" (3:17), "see to it" (Col. 2:8), "set your hearts" and "set your minds" (3:1–2).

By encouraging serious reflection upon God's character and will, the apostles were following the example of Jesus. When he was in the wilderness of Judea for forty days engaged in prayer, he was also engaged in thinking through what being the Messiah would mean in the context of the Judaism of his day. And the testing he faced and the temptations that came to him are to be viewed as being closely related to this meditation which flowed into and out of his prayer and communion with the Father. His teaching bears the marks of someone who has thought deeply and profoundly upon God's character and will, and upon how this applies to daily living; thus we are to understand that, like the psalmist, he meditated by day and by night upon the revealed will of God. We are given glimpses of this practice when the Gospels tell us that he arose early to pray, or that he walked on ahead of the disciples, deep in thought. Further, in his teaching, he encouraged people to reflect upon God's revelation and to live in the light of serious reflection. For example, in the Sermon on the Mount he told his disciples to look at God's provision in nature and draw deductions from it: "*Look* at the birds of the air . . . *See* how the lilies of the field grow . . ." (Mt. 6:26ff.). Then, in the parables, he called upon people to take up the insight which he offered through a short story or illustration and think about it, with a view to action. "He who has ears, let him hear" (Mt. 13:9), and after he has understood, let him do the will of God.

The Historical Precedent

In the light of the great emphasis within the Bible upon reflection, consideration, serious thought and careful enquiry, it is not surprising that great weight has been placed on meditation within the Church over the centuries. This emphasis is found in the Eastern Orthodox, Roman Catholic and Protestant traditions.[1] In the early Church, within the monastic life, there developed the practice of *lectio* (reading the Bible), *meditatio* (reflection and consideration) and *oratio* (prayer). Each led into the other, and thus this method was followed during each of the daily acts of worship. Something like this is still practiced by people, inside and outside religious houses, who use a daily office.

Then, also, *contemplatio* was encouraged. This was possible at any time or place and involved the recalling of one or another aspect of God's revelation or grace (e.g., the agony of Christ in the Garden of Gethsemane), followed by serious and individual reflection upon this, applying it to personal faith and circumstances. Apart from meditation that rose from the reading of the daily portion of the Scriptures, or meditation or contemplation that arose by individual choice in the personal search for communion with the living God, some people engaged in forms of meditation which amounted to serious reflection upon their lives and how they had ignored or responded to the grace of God. Such meditations were spread over several or many weeks; the most famous is that of Augustine of Hippo, available as a book entitled *The Confessions of St. Augustine.*

The meditation or contemplation which I am seeking to encourage can be either that which arises from reading the sacred Scriptures in a spirit of prayer and humility, or that which arises from recalling one or another aspect of God's grace and revelation. In particular, what is being emphasized is that to meditate regularly upon the heavenly realm, where Christ is, is not only beneficial but also necessary for all Christians. In adopting such a position, we are following in the paths established not only by the early Church but also by that great Bible-expositor and reformer John Calvin (1509–1564) and the authentic Protestant tradition. In his *Institutes of the Christian Religion,* which is one of the few really great accounts of Christianity for the ordinary believer, Calvin insists that meditation or contemplation is a necessary part of the Christian life; further, he insists that meditation upon the heavenly and future life is a duty of Christians as they journey through this world as pilgrims towards the heavenly Jerusalem.[2]

For Calvin an important aspect of meditating on the life of heaven is to compare soberly the glory, stability and joy of the heavenly life with the comparative poverty, uncertainty and misery of life in this world. If this comparison is made soberly and sincerely, Calvin held, it will help to create within believers a proper attitude (he used the word *contemptio*—"contempt") towards this world and its supposed glories, as well as putting us in the right attitude both to bear its miseries and to indulge in its pleasures. In the *Institutes* he wrote: "If heaven is our country, what can earth be but a place of exile? If departure from the world is entrance into life, what is the world but a sepulcher, and what is residence in it but immersion in death? . . . Thus when the earthly is compared with the heavenly life, the former may undoubtedly be despised and trampled underfoot."[3] Meditation for Calvin implies not only the exercise of the reasoning mind but also the exercising of desire and aspiration. It is, in other words, the work of the whole soul and is not merely a cerebral exercise. We are to meditate upon the heavenly and future life with our whole soul and heart, not merely with our intellect. Only such true and holy thinking about the exalted Christ will lift us up to him to behold his grace and glory.

It is easy to dismiss the insights of Calvin, and those saints and theologians before and after him, by stating that it was easy for them to have *contemptio* for the world. Did they not live in times when more babies died in infancy than survived? Were they not regularly subject to the ravages of disease and plague? Was not their life expectancy much less than ours, and was not the provision for their bodily health and happiness so much less than that which is made for us today? Because of the uncertainty of life and the frequency of early death, it was easy, it is claimed, for them to have "contempt" for the world; but for us, who expect to live longer and are surrounded by so many amazing achievements of science and technology, it is not so easy—indeed it is wrong—to have contempt for the world.

Let us be clear how the word "world" is being used here by Calvin (as he follows St. John, who taught, "Love not the world . . ."). It is not the world as God intended it to be when he created it; rather, it is the world as it exists, seriously affected by sin and in moral disorder; it is the world infected by pride, because human beings refuse to accept that they are creatures whose duty it is to worship and obey God and thus enjoy his blessings; and it is a world of covetousness, where people desire what they do not truly need and what is not in the long run good for them. Those who aspire to heaven must have "contempt" for this world, even if they are to live in it for seventy or more years, and they must look to that world which will replace this world when the new creation is revealed at the Last Day.

Of course, we are to have a positive attitude towards the world in which we live, for despite its fallen condition, it is God's creation, which still reveals his character and glory for those with eyes to see. As one writer puts it:[4]

What is our attitude to this world to be? Treat it as if it is all there is and as if all that you need is to be found in it, and it will dangle its gifts before your eyes, decoy you, tantalize you, and finally mock and desert you, leaving you empty-handed and with ashes in your mouth. But treat it as the creation of God, as truly good because it is God's handiwork and yet not the highest good because it is not God himself, live in this world as one who knows that the world is God's and yet as one who knows that his true home is not here but in eternity, and the world itself will yield up to you its joys and splendors of whose existence the mere worldling is utterly ignorant. Then you will see the world's transience and fragility, its finitude and its powerlessness to satisfy, not as signs that life is a bad joke with man as the helpless victim, but as pale and splintered reflections of the splendor and beauty of the eternal God—that beauty ever old and ever new—in whom alone man can find lasting peace and joy.

Taking his advice to heart, we can now proceed to identify the steps into meditation on the heavenly realm.

Steps into Meditation

In taking these steps, we shall allow ourselves to be guided by the recommendations provided in *The Saints' Everlasting Rest* by Richard Baxter. These represent the best Protestant adaptation of the approach to meditation inherited from the medieval and early Church. Baxter insisted that as bodily digestion turns food into energy for vigorous health, so meditation turns the truth received from Scripture into warm affection, firm resolutions and holiness of life. He emphasized, and in this he presented the best Protestant tradition, that meditation is "the acting of all the powers of the soul"; in other words, it involves and includes the intellect, feelings and will. Mind and heart and will are all involved.

Therefore, meditation is not to be confused with rigorous theological thinking—e.g., on the relation of time and eternity or on the relation between earth and heaven—and also it is not to be confused with feelings of elation or ecstasy—e.g., when you really feel that God loves you, really you. Meditation requires the use of the intellect and it involves the feelings, but it is the combination of intellect, heart and feelings, and determination and will which constitutes its real nature.

Before proceeding to the inner preparation for meditation, something must be said about its context. Effective meditation can only be pursued in a quiet place, on a regular basis and at an appropriate time of day or night. Here, getting into good habits is of great importance, since when resolution is weak the possession of a good habit often guarantees that duty is done.

Jesus himself retired to a quiet hillside, a lonely wilderness, a solitary garden or a closed room in order to meditate and pray. Isaac went out into the fields in the evening (Gen. 24:63). I find it best to retire to my study. Many people today go into their bedrooms. The important point is that it is a place that is quiet and where there will be no interruptions. For a few—e.g., hard-pressed mothers—meditation in the night as they lie in their beds may be the only option.

As to frequency, nothing less than once a day is sufficient. This is demanding, as I know from my own experience. It is so easy to neglect, forget, put off or postpone it and so lose or never attain daily frequency. However, if you ponder this requirement, you will see why. Like any other spiritual or bodily discipline, it is true that while practice does not make perfect, it certainly causes you to be much more proficient than you would be without that practice. Further, since the purpose of Christian meditation is to bring you close to God, to be truly acquainted with him, and to have communion with him, then, unless you meet him regularly in this exercise, he will be as a stranger to you when you seek to find him on the rare or intermittent occasions when you do meditate.

Over and above this daily norm, there are special days—e.g., each Lord's Day and special Christian festivals—and certain periods when you will be well advised to give yourself to extra meditation. On the Lord's Day we hope to experience a foretaste of heaven in the corporate worship and fellowship in which we engage. Why should we not also set apart time to fix our hearts and minds on things above? Then in times of great joy when you have experienced great blessing from God, you ought, as it were, to capitalize on this blessing by contemplating the greater blessings that are in store for you in heaven. And meditation is so necessary when you are going through a period of great distress or trial, for you can contemplate how Jesus came to his joy and reward through the path of trial and suffering. Finally, we ought to encourage all elderly Christians frequently to meditate upon that country into which they soon will be admitted: in this way their death will truly be a joyous occasion. There is, regrettably, a developing tendency these days to refuse to speak of one's death; Christians ought not to fall prey to this tendency but face death as the open door into the presence of the living God and into the Church triumphant in heaven.

The soul has to be prepared for meditation, just as the piano has to be tuned in order to play sweet music.

Because prayer and meditation belong closely together, preparation to meditate is much the same as to pray. First of all, you must lay aside thoughts which have been running through your mind in the immediate past—thoughts of family, of business, of education, of health, of church matters, of pleasure and leisure. Say to yourself, "I want to seek the Lord with my whole soul, with my understanding, heart and will," and persuade yourself that this is possible. "With Christ's help all things are possible and I shall devote my whole soul to this meditation." And in the second place, you must tell yourself, and become wholly aware, of the solemnity and seriousness of that in which you are to engage. Recall that you are to meditate upon the revelation of the Lord in the presence of the Lord. Say to yourself: "I look for the awakening of my drowsy spirit, of being aroused by God's holy presence and being overwhelmed by the sight of his Majesty and glory." Go forward into meditation desirous of being humble, reverent and teachable in your encounter with the living God.

Consideration

The key word which describes how meditation proceeds is "consideration." Let us suppose that you have chosen to meditate upon the theme of the exaltation of Jesus Christ to the right hand of the Father. Thus you will have a rich store of information in your mind about what the Scriptures state concerning the Resurrection. Ascension and Coronation of Jesus and of his sitting at the right hand of the Father in heaven. (Meditation is of course only possible when you have previously made efforts to receive and understand the teaching of the New Testament, the Creeds and the essentials of the Christian tradition. For this reason the first part of this book has been aimed primarily at the understanding and intellect.) Consideration is the way by which you open the door between your understanding and your affections, between your head and your heart. "He is usually the best scholar, whose apprehension is quick, clear and tenacious: but, he is usually the best Christian, whose apprehension is the deepest, and most affectionate, and who has the readiest passage, not so much from the ear to the brain, as from the brain to the heart. And though the Holy Spirit be the principal cause: yet, on our part, this passage must be opened by consideration.[5] There is much that goes by the name of meditation today that is purely an exercise of the intellect and understanding. We want it to be an exercise of the whole soul, enhancing the character and personality.

To consider is the way to reason with, and persuade, your heart to desire the heavenly realm and to be heavenly minded. Consideration causes your will to begin to act in line with your citizenship in heaven. From your memory you are to bring forth all the reasons you can muster as to why heaven is supremely important for you. This exercise will, in fact, be a kind of reading over to yourself of God's reasons supplied within his Revelation, which you have read and are constantly reading and digesting. In this book we have noted many of these reasons: for example, that any earthly treasure, however wonderful, is temporal and ultimately unsatisfying, whereas heavenly treasure is eternal and totally satisfying. Now you may find that this exercise of recalling and putting to yourself, as forcibly as you know how, God's reasons why heaven should be the center of your thought and affections is exhausting—at least until you get into the regular habit of doing it. If this is your experience, the reason is that you have allowed the muscles of your soul to become flabby or weak through not exercising them!

Having recalled the biblical descriptions of Christ in heaven and also the promises concerning your already being in him there as well as actually going to him there, you are then to exercise your judgment upon this information as you also heartily believe in the truth of what you have recalled. You are to do such mental acts as—surveying the biblical material and recognizing the supreme quality of celestial happiness; determining that by the grace of God this is the happiness that you and your loved ones (and as many as you can persuade) will actually enjoy; admiring the plan and purpose of God, who in grace has provided such a place and sphere with such a Savior and Lord for sinners such as you are; and being deeply grateful that this world with all its sin and suffering will be replaced at the end of the age by a new world without such things but filled with joy and love. You will feel that your heart is moving towards heaven as by faith you grasp the promises and consider their implications for you. Here faith and hope, sustained by the Holy Spirit, combine.

Your love for God will be enriched and enhanced as you are moved by the recollection and sight (by faith) of his love for you in raising you with and in Christ to the heavenly realm. As you see how the righteous angels worship and praise the Lord in pure love of his holy name, you too will want to express your love to God by praising him and magnifying his grace. When you hear the exalted Lord saying to you (as he did to peter—Jn. 21:15ff.), "Do you love me?," without any hesitation you sincerely respond, "Yes, Lord, I do love you." And you will praise him the more.

As your heart is fixed on things above, you will perhaps say something like the following to yourself: "What have I seen? Such beauty, such glory, such perfection, such amazing grace. O that I could see heaven a thousand times more clearly! O that I were there to join that heavenly company! O that I could partake of that great Feast! O that I were free from this mortal body and in my resurrection body to participate wholly in the life of heaven!" And thus you will feel your heart moving in desire towards that same Reality to which already your thoughts aspire.

Love and longing, praise and desire, will help you to strengthen your hope so you will leave your meditation fortified to face temptation and trial. Recite for your own benefit all the reasons why you should live in hope of what you have only seen by faith; it is God who has promised and has called you in faith and hope to be his child, and this is the God who has raised Jesus from the dead and placed him on his throne in heaven. "Why should I not hope? If God, who has given these promises, is on my side, who can effectively oppose me or stand in the way of their fulfillment and fruition?"

As your hope is fortified, so also will be your joy in the Lord and your courage to go and do his will whatever it costs. As you consider that the exalted Lord Jesus sends his Spirit to live within you, to guide you, to help you to pray and to witness, you will say to yourself: "Whom or what should I fear? Is not the presence of Almighty God with me, and if so, why should I not be bold in his name for the sake of the Gospel?" And as you look forward in hope and upward in faith and desire, your heart will ring with joy and you will know why the apostle urged: "Rejoice in the Lord always. I will say it again: Rejoice!" (Phil. 4:4).

Meditation begins with the mind, moves into the heart and sets you on course for doing God's will day by day. It can, as we have said, so easily move into prayer—prayer of penitence for lack of faith, hope and love; of praise and adoration of our great Lord; of thanksgiving for his mercies; and so on. But it is important that you do actually make time for meditation and do practice this discipline, since it is one sure way, if properly done, of taking God's truth not only into your heart but also into your daily life.

To consider is at the center of effectual meditation, and this is an act of the soul of which we are all capable; it is not to be seen as only possible by those who have reached a certain educational standard at school, college or university. However, as was admitted above, this God-given (Holy Spirit–assisted) activity is something that all Christians (except they be mentally sick or subnormal) are capable of, since "to consider" is part of the natural endowment of our souls.

Finally, if it be the case, as we have insisted, that meditation upon heaven (of which we have given merely one example of one starting point) is chiefly to be encouraged, this in no way means that meditations upon any of the multitude of aspects of God's revelation and grace should not also be engaged in. Of course they should be, as long as meditation on the heavenly realm has the prime place.

It ought to have the prime place because of the

simple fact that Christ is there and not anywhere else. He is our exalted King, Priest and Prophet, and we are in him by faith and love, and going to him in hope and obedience. We come to God in, by and through him, and God reveals himself to us and gives us grace uniquely in Jesus. He is the First and the Last, the Beginning and the End.

Utilizing the Physical Senses

Those who have tried to engage in this kind of demanding meditation usually come to the conclusion that it is much easier to either talk or preach about heaven, or to think intellectually about the doctrine of heaven, than it is to meditate with the heart. Yet we pray: "May the words of my mouth and the meditation of my heart be pleasing in your sight O LORD" (Ps. 19:14).

However, since we are endowed with our physical senses, it is wise to call them into use in our meditation so that our task becomes easier and more pleasant and we are better able to concentrate. Richard Baxter has some useful suggestions to offer in this area and so I shall make use of them.

First of all, you are to think of the joys above in heaven as boldly as the scriptural writers have presented them. You must not believe that you have to think abstractly and in highly conceptual ways. Think of Christ as you believe he looked when he ascended into heaven in the sight of his disciples; think of the glorified saints in heaven as human beings made perfect and supremely happy: do not hesitate to take a mental journey with John, who wrote the last book of the

Bible. Let him conduct you around the heaven that he saw and along the roads of the heavenly Jerusalem. Listen to the songs of the angels as they join together to praise the Lord and the Lamb, and see Christ seated upon his throne. Having seen and heard, then feel the peace and the joy of that place and you will be uplifted in spirit. Tell yourself that soon you will be there to enter into that joy, and imagine what that experience will be like.

Secondly, do not hesitate boldly to compare the objects of sense with the objects of faith in order to recognize the infinite superiority of the latter. See people having a great dinner party, enjoying their food and wine, and compare this to the heavenly and messianic feast which will be in heaven: how much more wonderful to feed upon Christ the living bread than to eat the best food available on earth! See people enjoying the benefits of wealth, honor and position and compare this with the enjoyment of the beatific vision of God the Holy Trinity, and the fellowship of the saints and angels in heaven. Listen to your favorite music, which is so moving and soothing, and compare it with the music of the heavenly choirs, who bow before the Lord in adoration and praise. Look upon the beautiful sights in nature and compare them with the beauty and glory that belong to God and his heaven. If what you can see, hear and smell can be so wonderful and beautiful, how much more will be the wonder and beauty of heaven.

In the third place, compare the delights of heaven with the delight experienced in the discovery of new knowledge or information. There is great delight for a child as he or she discovers the truths of mathematics and science, just as there is delight for scientists when they believe they have discovered a new law of nature or for theologians when they believe they have penetrated more deeply into the mystery of the Truth, who is God. Heaven will be one exciting journey into the Reality of God, with new discoveries of the riches of his character and grace a constant delight in the move from glory into more glory. Heaven will be a growth into the inexhaustible and holy love of God, that love which binds Father, Son and Holy Spirit as One God. If the discovery of knowledge about the temporal and finite brings such joy, how much more will the discovery of the eternal and infinite.

Fourthly, compare the joy and provision of heaven with what you have known in the fellowship and worship of your church and in private devotions. Think of how your heart has been warmed, and your mind has been stimulated, and your will has been fired through various experiences. Think of how, at times, you have been lost to the world because you have been caught up in wonder, love and praise. Recall how you have had peace in the midst of great problems, and joy when you were sorely tried and tested. Then imagine that your life in heaven will be a constant experience of warmth, stimulation, desire to serve, and being lost in wonder, love and praise. Here you only read the book of Isaiah and sing the songs of the psalmists and study the Sermon on the Mount and try your best to understand Paul's teaching; there you will meet Isaiah, the psalmists and Paul, and with them you will join in the praise of Jesus, the Lamb and the Son. Read over again or recall what happened when Jesus was transfigured (Mt. 17:1–13). The disciples were so overcome with that supernatural experience that they wanted it to last forever—"it is good for us to be here," they said. They had only a foretaste of heaven: How much more would they have tried to remain had it been heaven itself?

Finally, compare your mortal body with the resurrected body of Christ and recall that you are to be given a body like his glorious body. Now you may be pretty or handsome, strong or weak, attractive or ugly, but you do know within your heart the impulses of the Holy Spirit as he witnesses with your spirit that you are a child of God and can truly call him "Father." Yet this body of yours is subject to all kinds of problems— even when it is tended by the best doctors using the best medicine; and your mind is subject to all kinds of problems as well—even when it is cared for by the best psychiatrist using the latest techniques. Think of Christ in his glorified body, that body which is in a state of everlasting perfection and free from the possibility of all pain and decay, in and through which the Holy Spirit freely and fully moves. Consider that you also will soon enjoy this experience when there is no war within you between the flesh and the spirit, when your body and your soul function in perfect harmony in the service of the Lord.

All this is good advice, you may say, but what am I to do about my wandering thoughts? The answer is that you are to say to yourself something like this: "I am a Christian: God has placed his Spirit in my heart; in the name of Christ and with help of the Spirit I can do what is right and acceptable before God." Be firm with yourself and see yourself as truly a child of God, loved by your heavenly Father and assisted by his grace. Then call upon your heavenly Father and your exalted Savior, saying something like this: "Father, you have endowed me with reason, which is to have command over my thoughts, affections and feelings. This authority of reason is given by you in order that I might do your will. You tell me to engage in meditation upon heaven, but my thoughts and feelings rebel and go off in other directions. Assist me, O my God, to exercise my reason and control my affections. O send your Spirit upon me that I may do what you command, even as the Lord Jesus did what you commanded. Amen." Believing that God is wholly on your side in this matter, then begin again: truly meditate.

Be aware that a common temptation is to cease your meditation when it is just really beginning to lift you up to heaven. You will, as it were, come to the sight of the land of promise, be thrilled with the sight, and then feel so satisfied as to jump up and lose your concentration. Do not be satisfied with the mere sight—however wonderful it is—but press on till you actually enter the promised land and see its glory, feel its warmth, and desire to stay there forever.

Perhaps this is the point to put down this book and resolve to have a go before you do anything else. In learning to ride a bicycle, the child needs to persevere and pick himself up often from his falls. So in the discipline and exercise of meditation, especially upon the heavenly realm, you need to persevere and be ready to pick yourself up often and begin again until you have acquired and maintain the art and discipline.

9. Practical Benefits

Today, many Christians want to know what difference believing in this or that teaching or doctrine makes to their lives. Unless they can see obvious and immediate calculable benefits, they tend to reject, or have little enthusiasm for considering, the teaching. In anticipation that the same question is asked of the practice of meditation, here are some of the practical benefits experienced by those who, being born from *above* (Jn. 3:1–8), sincerely meditate on *things above*.

These may be divided for the sake of clarity into three kinds: (a) growing in holiness, (b) witnessing in the world and (c) attitude towards God. Naturally, what is said under one heading probably also has implications under the others.

Holiness[1]

Wherever you are and whatever you do, you cannot evade or avoid temptations to sin. They occur when you least expect them, and unless you are spiritually alert and fortified, then you will fall to their power. If your heart is frequently in heaven in contemplation, then what the tempter offers to you will always seem inferior and what he seeks to persuade you to do will always appear unacceptable. You will say to Satan: "Get behind me, Satan: do not try to persuade me to forsake my Lord for trifling and transient pleasures which cannot satisfy me. What will be my profit if I gain the whole world and lose my inheritance in heaven? Be gone!"

And remember that at the bottom of the mountain the impatient Israelites could not resist temptation and fell into idolatry; but Moses, his face shining with the encounter with heaven, stood firm (Ex. 32). Consider also that on the Mount of Transfiguration when Peter beheld the glory of Jesus as he conversed with Elijah and Moses, he was unlikely to fall into temptation; however, later, when his eyes were not upon that glory, he could not resist temptation when his Master was facing his great ordeal (Mt. 17:1–8; 26:69–75).

Then, however strong your faith, you will ask from time to time: "What assurance do I have that I am a real Christian? How do I know that I am being made holy by the indwelling Spirit?" The answer which you provide for yourself will include reminding yourself of the precious and rich promises contained within the Gospel of the kingdom of God, of the internal witness of the Spirit with your Spirit that you are a child of

God and do address him sincerely as "Father," and of your true desire to love your Christian brothers and sisters as well as all your neighbors. It should also include the confirming to yourself that you do really and truly desire to have treasure in heaven and that you do—if *not* all the time, then some of the time— long to be there. Did not Jesus teach that "where your treasure is, there your heart will be also" (Mt. 6:21)? A heart set upon heaven, that is, upon the living God, is truly a heart which is the recipient of saving grace. Your own heart, in its aspirations for Christ who is above, will be for you a sincere confirmation that you are a child of God and on the heavenly way.

And if your life is like that of most people, you are going to face illness and disease (especially as you get older), as well as tragedy, trial and mental pain through events over which you have no personal control. At such times, and in such periods, you will certainly find that your acquaintance with heaven and your Lord above will be precious. We have a High Priest in Jesus who is able to sympathize with our weaknesses, and with his help you can put into the perspective of heaven (a very different one from that of earth!) these difficulties and thereby continue your pilgrimage heavenward over and through this rough terrain.

The psalmist knew how to look to heaven in times when everything seemed dark and difficult: "One thing I ask of the LORD, this is what I seek: that I may dwell in the house of the LORD all the days of my life, to gaze upon the beauty of the LORD and to seek him in his temple. For in the day of trouble he will keep me safe in his dwelling; he will hide me in the shelter of his tabernacle and set me high upon a rock . . ." (Ps. 27:4–5). Too many of us seem to lose faith and hope in difficult periods; if our hearts were more in heaven, we would increase our faith and hope in such times.

God calls us to be holy even as he is holy. God calls us to be set apart from sin and wholly dedicated to his service both while we are here on earth and when we enter into the liberty of the kingdom of heaven of the age to come. To the extent that our hearts are frequently in heaven, we shall see and know his holiness and thus desire to participate in it and reflect it. There is no growth in holiness on earth unless first a vision of, and a participation in, God's holiness is received from heaven in prayerful, humble meditation.

Witness to the World[2]

Jesus calls his disciples to be the "salt of the earth" (Mt. 5:13). Salt is still a basic commodity. It is essentially different in taste from the food into which it is put and is therefore able to change the taste of the whole. Its effectiveness lies in its quality and in its difference, and these point to your role in the world as a follower of the Lord Jesus. Further, salt is used to preserve meat from decay, and this points to your role in the Church and the world in maintaining God's standards and imparting his values. If your heart is regularly in heaven, your quality and power as salt will be maintained.

Jesus also calls his disciples to be the "light of the world" (Mt. 5:14–16) and to follow him, for he is "the light" from where then light comes (Jn. 8:12). For light to be effective in dispelling darkness, it must be placed in a strategic position; and, of course, light is truly appreciated as light when it enters darkness. If your heart is regularly in heaven, then you will be filled with the light of Christ, and this will be reflected not only in what you say but in what you are.

Paul told the church in Corinth that as a fellowship and as individual Christians they were, as "a letter from Christ" to be read by the people among whom they lived and worked (2 Cor. 3:2–3). If your heart is regularly in heaven, then, as a letter to be read, the message written in your character and behavior will be the clearer, proclaiming Christ who is in heaven and present by the Holy Spirit within you.

Those with pink or white skins who go in search of the sun come back browned or reddened in face and body; those with open hearts who go in search of the Lord in meditation return changed people who are not only ready but also empowered to go forth into the world as witnesses. Such people do not necessarily talk more intellectually of the God whom they know, but they do certainly talk more familiarly and reverently of him, his grace, salvation and his heaven. The secret of having great energy for the Lord in his world as his witness is to spend much time with him in meditation and prayer. The heavenly minded Christian is the truly lively Christian; he or she is not dull and does not do merely what is expected of him or her; but he or she is brave for God, doing the unexpected and the unlikely as the Spirit directs and leads.

If you are a zealous person, ask from where your zeal comes. Is it from reading certain exciting books? Is it from the influence of an eloquent preacher? Is it from the dynamism of a charismatic fellowship? Or is it from some other source? The zeal which is the most likely to be heavenly zeal, the zeal of the "Lord of hosts," is that which is kindled and fired by your heavenly meditation. This is not to downgrade the others but to insist that nothing can be a substitute for the daily ascent of the heavenly mount to be warmed by the celestial fire.

Attitude Towards God[3]

The first of the ten commandments is "You shall have no other gods before me" (Dt. 5:7). We have learned that idols need not be the gods of Hinduism or Greek mythology but are for us parts of, or aspects of, contemporary, technological society. Indeed, to speak metaphorically, there are in Western society many idols for destruction. Then the Lord who forbids idolatry also calls us to love him with all our heart, soul, mind and strength. We have learned that this is an impossibility as long as we are in these mortal bodies with our sinful human natures. The command is always before us as the goal at which we aim. It is those who are often with the Lord in sincere meditation who are most aware of the idolatry they must avoid and the love they must offer; it is those who have been with the adoring heavenly host who are most desirous of living on earth as the saints and angels live in heaven. What heavenly meditation does for the sincere soul is increase its capacity for praise.

Have you known the experience of being temporarily

overcome by a sense of the admirability of a great painting or sculpture, or by the beauty of a piece of music? If you have, you will know what is the nature of praise, the praise of the angels and saints in heaven who call out, "Holy, holy, holy is the Lord . . ." and "Worthy is the Lamb . . ." (Rev. 4:8; 5:12). Like the psalmist, you will want to say to your fellow believers: "Sing joyfully to the LORD, you righteous: it is fitting for the upright to praise him" (Ps. 33:1).

Praising the Lord has a paradoxical character. "The sole justification for praising God is that God is praise-worthy. We do not praise God because it does us good, though no doubt it does. We do not praise God because it does him good, for in fact it does not. Praise is thus strictly ecstatic, in the sense that it takes us wholly out of ourselves; it is purely and solely directed upon God."[4]

Now this kind of argument is not much heard in contemporary Christianity. Everything seems to have to be justified on the basis of its practical effects. But your highest and noblest activity as a Christian can only be justified on the basis that you have seen the Lord; and what you have seen and what you therefore know cause you to desire to praise him—and praise him, and praise him. Fresh from your heavenly meditation, you want your whole life to be characterized by the praise of God.

> Fill thou my life O Lord my God in every part with praise
> That my whole being might proclaim thy being and thy ways.

We have been saved to live to the praise of God's glory (Eph. 1:12). And, on earth, there is nothing more wonderful than a company of Christians whose hearts have been recently in heaven joining together to sing praises to God. Faith and hope will not be needed in the kingdom of heaven of the age to come; but there your love will be magnified and enriched. Praise will be your primary employment in heaven, and the more you are familiar with heaven on earth, the more will you praise the Lord here below. In fact, your love will be purified by your praising of the Lord as you make your pilgrimage heavenward.

Epilogue

I bring this book to a close with a meditation. I hope that the reading of it will give you some idea as to what is involved in this spiritual discipline. However, it must be made clear that all that can be communicated in the written word is the first part of the whole task of meditation: this is because only *you* can feel in your heart the force of the truth that your mind is apprehending and only *you* can determine in your will to live by that truth.

The meditation is based upon the closing words of that great book, *The City of God*, written by Augustine of Hippo early in the fifth century. The original Latin is as follows: *"Vacabimus et videbimus, videbimus et amabimus, amabimus et laudabimus. Ecce quod erit in fine sine fine."* In heaven "we shall rest and we shall see; we shall see and we shall love; we shall love and we shall praise. Behold, what shall be in the end shall never end." This is a fine summary of the biblical insights into our life in heaven and is thus a worthy basis for contemplation of the heavenly life.

We

Heaven is, and will be, community, the communion of the saints. From the old and new covenants, from every continent and race, from all classes and types of human beings, we shall be together as the perfected people of God. We shall spend eternity getting to know one another and celebrating the grace of God in all our lives. We shall not be divided by doctrine, ceremonial or ritual; we shall not be estranged by the barriers of sin: for we shall be the family of God in our Father's presence, living as his adopted, trusting and grateful children, serving him in one another. All together we shall rest and we shall see, we shall see and we shall love, we shall love and we shall praise; and this experience will be forever and will get the richer as we go forward into it.

We Shall Rest (Vacabimus)

We shall be on a permanent vacation or holiday in heaven in our Father's presence. Now we are engaged in warfare, fighting valiantly under the banner of Christ against sin, the world and the devil; this service as soldiers and servants of Christ must continue to the end of our lives, and we must not be ashamed to confess the faith of Christ, crucified and risen. In heaven we shall rest from this spiritual warfare.

We live in a world where suffering is usually not far away—if not within the family, then made real by vivid images on the TV screen. Though modern medicine helps to remove bodily pain, yet many seem to suffer mental and spiritual pain. And we live in a world where we are allowing ourselves to become more and more dependent upon technological aids and to the seemingly inevitable fact they will be out of date before we have fully used them. In heaven we shall rest from pain, suffering and sadness; in heaven we shall find that all that we truly want and need will be everlasting.

Resting and vacationing are not merely being away from that which tires and wearies, saddens and depresses. We know from experience how exhilarating and invigorating a vacation can be. We shall enter into God's own Sabbath-rest, which is certainly not into inertia and boredom. God, in his infinite being, both rests and works (maintaining his creation); he rests by contemplating what he has made—what is meant to be and how it will be—and this contemplation satisfies his eternal mind. Rest is perfect and unruffled life, and this will be our inheritance as we, too, are wholly satisfied and fulfilled as we "vacation" in our contemplation of God—of what he has done, is doing and shall do for us. And we shall enter into this rest even as we also serve the Lord in ways which now we cannot imagine or know; like God himself, we shall both rest and work simultaneously, and we shall never get bored or tired.

We Shall Rest and We Shall See
(Vacabimus et Videbimus)

In our contemplation of God's creation we shall also see God; we shall enjoy the beatific vision and we shall be wholly content and blessed.

We see now with our physical eyes God's creation; though it is hard in our Western culture to see the cosmos as reflecting God's eternal power and glory, yet from time to time we do enjoy insights into the creative power of God as we survey the created order. Occasionally we have a sense of wonder and feel great reverence. Yet we know that as creatures of space and time we cannot see with these eyes of ours God as he really is: we can see what he has made and we can have a sense of his presence in and around us. The ancient Israelites enjoyed special signs of God's presence—e.g., in the luminous cloud that descended upon the Tabernacle and Temple—but they recognized that no man could actually see God and come from that experience alive. The sights of God which Moses and others were given are to be compared to the sight of the afterglow in the west when the sun has gone down.

Apart from our physical eyes, we do have the "eyes" of our heart and mind by which we can see and know spiritual reality. The disciples saw God in the person and ministry of Jesus, and we, too, as careful students of the Gospels, can see God in Jesus. We see in this way because we also believe and trust in God. Jesus promised that the pure in heart shall see God, and Paul spoke of an experience of being "face to face" with the Lord in heaven. In heaven we shall be in the presence of the LORD: we shall see the LORD in and through the

Incarnate Son; we shall more and more appreciate his character and will, his grace and glory, his creation and redemption. We shall grow ever more deeply in this appreciation as we see who the Lord is and what the Lord is to us. We shall see God in that the whole basis of our lives will be fellowship and communion with him through the Incarnate Son.

We Shall Rest and We Shall See; We Shall See and We Shall Love
(Videbimus et Amabimus)

As we see God, enjoying full communion with him, we shall love (*agapē*) him and we shall love our fellow saints. In our pilgrimage in this fallen world we have much-needed faith, hope and love; in heaven we shall be filled with the love of God, and in seeing him we shall not need faith and hope any longer. Our inheritance is the inheritance of the height and depth and length and breadth of the love of God and of Christ Jesus our Lord.

With the eyes of faith we see the love of God revealed at Calvary; with our physical eyes we see glimpses of pure, unselfish and compassionate love in certain human relationships and acts. And we know what misery and what despair are caused through the absence of real and true love in human relationships. We, therefore, find it hard to imagine what the effect of the presence of pure love in all the members of heaven will be on the relationships between the saints and between God and the saints.

We believe not only that we shall love and serve God

for God's own sake, but that we shall love ourselves and each other also for the sake of God. This is an experience of which we hardly yet have any intimation of experience, for we now seem only to love God for our own sake and to love ourselves and our loved ones for our and their own sakes. In heaven we shall have the desire and ability to admire and love everyone around us for the sake of Christ who died and rose from the dead for them.

We Shall Rest and We Shall See; We Shall See and We Shall Love; We Shall Love and We Shall Praise (Amabimus et Laudabimus)

In loving God we shall be adoring God, and in adoring God we shall praise him. "Alleluia" will be the great expression in heaven: we shall both enjoy and glorify God forever. Angels have been doing this from the moment that heaven and they were created by God; we shall join in and extend their everlasting song.

As we love God for his own sake, we shall find ourselves ever praising him, for he is wholly and entirely praiseworthy. As we truly see him and know him, we shall be absolutely sure that he is totally admirable and therefore worthy of praise. We shall praise him for what he has done for us, but our fundamental reason why we shall praise him without ceasing is that we shall find him completely praiseworthy in himself. We shall not ask, "Why should I praise him?," because seeing him will be more than sufficient to set us off, and to maintain us, in the everlasting song of praise to Father, Son and Holy Spirit.

Behold, What Shall Be in the End Shall Never End
(Ecce Quod Erit in Fine Sine Fine)

Our resting, seeing, loving and praising belong together, and they will not only last forever, but they will expand, deepen and extend as we, the adopted family of God and the body of Christ, move from glory into more glory in the life of the kingdom of heaven of the age to come. Thanks be to God.

Since this is our great hope and inheritance, let us determine to live on earth as those who long to be in their true homeland and who know that their status is ever that of pilgrims and aliens on earth.

*   *   *

Richard Baxter's "Plea For Inspiration"

Ye holy Angels bright,
Who wait at God's right hand,
Or through the realms of light
Fly at your Lord's command,
        Assist our Song,
        Or else the theme
        Too high doth seem
        For mortal tongue.

Ye blessed souls at rest,
Who ran this earthly race,
And now, from sin released,
Behold the Savior's Face,
        His praises sound,
        As in His light
        With sweet delight
        Ye do abound.

Ye saints, who toil below,
Adore your heavenly King,
And onward as ye go
Some joyful anthem sing:
    Take what He gives
    And praise Him still,
    Through good and ill,
    Who ever lives!

My soul, bear thou thy part,
Triumph in God above,
And with a well-tuned heart
Sing thou the songs of love!
    Let all thy days
    Till life shall end,
    Whate'er He send,
    Be filled with praise.

Notes

Introduction

1. See further: A. A. Hoekema, *The Bible and the Future* (Exeter: Paternoster, 1979), and Hans Küng, *Eternal Life?* (London: Collins, 1984).
2. See Anton Van der Walle, *From Darkness to the Dawn* (London: S.C.M., 1984), pp. 74ff., and Christopher Rowland, *Christian Origins* (London: S.P.C.K., 1985), Part 2.
3. For an enlightened introduction to this area, see *The Meaning of the Millennium, Four Views*, ed. R. G. Clouse (Madison, Wis.: I.V.P., 1979).
4. See further: Paul Badham, *Christian Beliefs about Life after Death* (London: S.P.C.K., 1978).

1. My Father, Your Father

1. In Matthew's Gospel the voice from heaven said: "This is my Son, whom I love; with him I am well pleased" (Mt: 3:17). Here the voice of the Father seems to be addressing those present, complementing the word to Jesus—as was the case at the Transfiguration (Mt. 17:5).

2. It is by Robert Butterworth, S.J., and is from his article, "Has Chalcedon a Future?" *The Month*, April 1977. For the original Greek text and translation, see R. V. Sellers, *The Council of Chalcedon* (London: S.P.C.K., 1961).

3. (a) Mk. 14:36 (b) Q: Mt. 6:9 (Lk. 11:2); 11:25–27 (Lk. 10:21–22) (c) Luke only: 23:34, 46 (d) Matthew only: 26:42 (3) Jn. 11:41; 12:27ff.; 17:1, 5, 11, 21, 24ff.

4. Joachim Jeremias, *New Testament Theology*, 1 (London: S.C.M., 1971), pp. 63–68. See also: Robert Hamerton-Kelly, *God the Father: Theology and Patriarchy in the Teaching of Jesus* (Philadelphia: Fortress Press, 1979).

5. Jeremias, op. cit., p. 67.

6. T. W. Manson, *The Teaching of Jesus* (London: C.U.P., 1963), p. 113.

2. Heaven: Past, Present, Future

1. See further: Austin Farrer, "Heaven and Hell," *Saving Belief* (London: Longmans, 1972).

2. Ibid., p. 145.

3. See further: D. M. Hay, *Glory at the Right Hand: Psalm 110 in Early Christianity* (New York: Abingdon, 1973).

4. In his commentary on *Acts* (Leicester: I.V.P. 1980), Howard Marshall offers a further suggestion: "The point must be that Stephen sees Jesus in his role as the Son of man; he sees him as the One who suffered and was vindicated by God (Lk. 9:22), i.e., as a pattern to be followed by Christian martyrs, but also as the One, who will vindicate in God's presence those who are not ashamed of Jesus and acknowledge their allegiance to him before men (Lk. 12:8)," p. 149.

5. See further: Peter Toon, *The Ascension of Our Lord* (Nashville: Thomas Nelson, 1984), pp. 63–66.

6. On this title of *kyrios*, see the article in *The New International Dictionary of New Testament Theology*, vol. 2, ed. Colin Brown (Exeter: Paternoster), pp. 508ff. (hereafter cited as *New Int. Dict. of N.T. Theol.*).

7. See the article on "Limbo," *New Catholic Encyclopedia*, vol. 8,

ed. W. J. MacDonald (New York: McGraw-Hill, 1967–1979),
pp. 726ff.

3. Treasure in Heaven

1. Jeremias, op. cit., pp. 193ff.
2. For extended studies of the Sermon on the Mount, see W. D.
   Davies, *The Setting of the Sermon on the Mount* (London:
   C.V.P., 1976), and the more recent R. A. Guelich, *The Sermon
   on the Mount* (Waco, Tex.: Word, 1982).
3. On the theme of righteousness, see John Reumann, *Righteousness in the New Testament* (Philadelphia: Fortress Press,
   1982).
4. The most recent study of apocalyptic literature is that by
   Christopher Rowland, *The Open Heaven* (London: S.P.C.K.,
   1982).
5. On the world to come in the teaching of Jesus, see L. Goppelt,
   Theology of the New Testament, vol. 1 (London: S.P.C.K.,
   1981), pp. 72ff.; cf. Jeremias, op. cit., pp. 97ff.
6. See further: C. Ryder Smith, *The Bible Doctrine of the Hereafter* (London: Epworth, 1985), pp. 227–228.
7. There are many good commentaries on John's Gospel. I have
   used those by Raymond E. Brown (2 vols., 1966, 1970), Barnabas
   Lindars (1972) and Leon Morris (1971).

4. Patient Hope

1. On the inner work of the Spirit, see Michael Green, *I Believe
   in the Holy Spirit* (London: Hodder, 1975), pp. 76ff.
2. For a thorough study of the theology of Paul, see Herman
   Ridderbos, *Paul: An Outline of His Theology* (London:
   S.P.C.K., 1977).
3. See the article on "Salvation," *New Int. Dict. of N.T. Theol.*,
   vol. 3, pp. 216ff.
4. Reumann, op. cit.
5. See the article on "Sanctification," *New Int. Dict. of N.T.
   Theol.*, vol. 2, pp. 223ff.
6. See the article on "Hope," *New Int. Dict. of N.T. Theol.*, vol.
   2, pp. 238ff.

7. Rom. 4:18 (twice); 5:2; 5:4; 5:5; 8:20; 8:24 (three times); 12:12; 15:4; 15:13 (twice); verb in 8:24; 8:25; 15:12; 15:24.

8. There is a good exposition of this passage in A. T. Lincoln, *Paradise Now and Not Yet* (London: C.U.P., 1981, pp. 59ff.

9. There are helpful commentaries by F. W. Beare (3rd ed., 1933) and R. P. Martin (1960).

10. There are helpful commentaries by E. Schweizer (1982) and R. P. Martin (1972).

11. There are helpful commentaries by C. L. Mitton (1976) and M. Barth (1974).

5. A Better Country

1. Useful commentaries on Hebrews are by F. F. Bruce (1965) and Raymond Brown (1982); cf. F. L. Horton, *The Melchizedek Tradition* (London: C.U.P., 1976).

2. There have been several shortened versions of Baxter's book produced since Victorian times. The one I have used was published in London in 1928 with a foreword by M. Monckton of Balliol College, Oxford. The easiest way to read the whole work is in the *Practical Works*, ed. William Orme, 1830.

3. See further: the chapter on Christ as Priest in P. Toon, *The Ascension of Our Lord.*

6. A Living and Purifying Hope

1. Helpful commentaries on 1 Peter include those by J. N. D. Kelly (1969) and C. E. B. Cranfield (1962).

2. The best modern commentary on 2 Peter and Jude is R. J. Bauckham (1983); but Michael Green's (1968) is still helpful, as is also that by J. N. D. Kelly (1969).

3. The commentary by Raymond E. Brown in the Anchor Bible series on the Johannine Epistles seems to be the best available.

7. Obstacles and Hindrances

1. See further: E. L. Mascall, *Theology and the Gospel of Christ* (London: S.P.C.K., 1977), and the short but significant *Jesus: Who He Is* (London: D.L.T., 1985).
2. For such an apology, see the two books by Stephen Travis: *I Believe in the Second Coming of Christ* (London: Hodder, 1982) and *Christian Hope and the Future of Man* (Leicester: I.V.P., 1980).
3. John Scott has tried to marry the gospel of the kingdom and social concern in his *Issues Facing Christians Today* (Basingstoke: Marshalls, 1984).
4. See further: Robert Banks, *The Tyranny of Time* (Exeter: Paternoster, 1983). We must not forget that we also have a noise problem—some people cannot stand quietness!

8. Meditation: What Is It?

1. There are some short, useful articles on meditation in *A Dictionary of Christian Spirituality*, ed. G. S. Wakefield (London: S.C.M., 1983).
2. Book III, chapter 9 of the *Institutes* is entitled "Meditation on the Future Life." The best edition of the *Institutes* is that edited by John T. McNeill in 2 vols. in the Library of Christian Classics, 1961.
3. *Institutes.* III, 9, i.
4. E. L. Mascall, *Grace and Glory* (London: S.P.C.K., 1975), p. 82. I have found this book most stimulating.
5. Baxter, op. cit., p. 191.

9. Practical Benefits

1. On holiness, see both Donald Nicholl, *Holiness* (London: D.L.T., 1981), and the older books of the same title by Bishop J. C. Ryle, often reprinted.
2. On witness, see David J. Bosch, *Witness to the World* (Basingstoke: Marshalls, 1980).
3. On attitude to God, see J. I. Packer, *Knowing God* (London: Hodder, 1973).
4. Mascall, op., cit., p. 63.